||| |||

Shooting the Rapids:
Effective Ministry in a Changing World

BROADMAN PRESS
Nashville, Tennessee

©Copyright 1990 ● Broadman Press
All rights reserved
4260-13
ISBN: 0-8054-6013-6
Dewey Decimal Classification: 253
Subject Heading: MINISTRY
Library of Congress Card Catalog Number: 89-15878
Printed in the United States of America

Library of Congress Cataloging-in-Publication Data

Shooting the rapids : effective ministry in a changing world / Fred
  W. Andrea, compiler.
    p. cm.
    ISBN: 0-8054-6013-6
    1. Pastoral theology. 2.Sociology, Christian.
  3. Christianity--20th century. I. Andrea, Fred W.
  BV4011.S487 1990
  253--dc20   89-15878
                                   CIP

||| |||

To
G. Willis Bennett
teacher, colleague, and brother,
for his thoroughgoing commitment
to effective Christian ministry
in a changing world.

CONTENTS

Contributors

W. Jere Allen
Director, Metropolitan Missions Department
Southern Baptist Home Mission Board
Atlanta, Georgia

George W. Bullard, Jr.
Director, Missions Division
General Baord of the South Carolina Baptist Convention
Columbia, South Carolina

Michael J. Clingenpeel
Pastor, Franklin Baptist Church
Franklin, Virginia

C. Anne Davis
Dean, School of Social Work
The Southern Baptist Theological Seminary
Louisville, Kentucky

Edward B. Freeman, Jr.
Pastor, Monument Heights Baptist Church
Richmond, Virginia

C. Welton Gaddy
Pastor, Highland Hills Baptist Church
Macon, Georgia

Roy E. Godwin
Director of Missions and Evangelism
District of Columbia Baptist Church
Washington, D.C.

Preface

by Roy Honeycutt

Shooting the rapids on a white-water stream is both exciting and frightening. When my daughter graduated from university last year she had only one request. She asked me to go white-water rafting. Always meeting the unexpected, racing down a white-water stream underscores the uncertainty of every new turn in the river. Boulders challenge the raft's passage. The raft itself hurtles along on top of rocky ledges and submerged stones unseen to the eye but hazardous to the raft.

Later a friend sent pictures of our raft at the peak of its thrust through churning, white water. Only then did I understand our experience was risky as well as enjoyable. Gazing at the pictures it dawned on me how treacherous were the waters and limited the passages between huge boulders. Despite those threats, rafting the turbulent water was thrilling and exciting. In retrospect, the expert guide transformed an otherwise dangerous trip into a beautiful summer adventure.

Reflecting on that experience suggests that this book bears an appropriate title: *Shooting the Rapids: Effective Ministry in a Changing World*. Constructive ministry in today's world has many parallels to "shooting the rapids."

First, the church in contemporary society is much like a raft plunging down a chute of white water raging with foam. At times one wonders if anyone controls the raft's direction. Perhaps no one is setting the course, we conclude in moments of depression. Are we helpless, captive victims of the rushing waters? Is someone handling the rudder, steering a stable and productive course? Is the guide's strength adequate to shove the raft away from a rocky cliff? Can he simultaneously reverse its direction to meet the next churning rapids?

Without exception, contemporary leadership in every organization today is "shooting the rapids." The good news for the church is that you can shoot the rapids. In our changing world an otherwise turbulent and dangerous journey can become a thrilling, exciting adventure.

Shooting the Rapids provides creative suggestions for effective ministry in a changing world. Moving the church off the plateau will thrust the people of God into tumultuous but promising adventures. Confronting change proactively with long-range planning will chart a workable course through turbulent times. The church in transition succeeds to the degree it uses all God's people. Such a church makes no distinction based on age, race, or gender. These and other chapter emphases in *Shooting the Rapids* provide excellent counsel for churches willing to ride white water while shooting the rapids.

Second, in the experience with my daughter, a seasoned guide made the difference. His knowledge of the river transformed an otherwise treacherous venture into an enjoyable graduation excursion. The ability of our guide was remarkable. He knew the river as he knew his home. His strength consistently overcame the powerful river. He was always daring, yet properly cautious. Knowing the risks of some rapids, he and other guides strung safety ropes below the rapids. Without our guide the trip downriver would have been a failure. With him the rafting experience remains a memorable highlight of a bright, summer day.

Leadership remains the transforming factor for the success of institutions whose mission requires them to "shoot the rapids." Decades ago I recall someone commenting in an address, "No institution is likely to rise higher than the quality of its leadership." Organizations in contemporary society must have superior white-water guides if they successfully shoot the rapids.

Such excellence characterizes the life of Dr. G. Willis Bennett, provost of The Southern Baptist Theological Seminary and William Walker Brookes, professor of Church and Community, to whom this book is dedicated. Dr. Bennett exemplifies the positive qualities of an experienced guide who shoots the rapids of church and community change with excitement and expertise. His career has focused primarily on the care of congregations and their effective outreach to local communities. Few, if any, are his equal as a creative guide leading churches through changing social circumstances. Under his tutelage hundreds of pastors and teachers worldwide are competently "shooting the rapids." They do so effectively and with confidence because of Dr. G. Willis Bennett's professional counsel and personal example as an effective minister of Jesus Christ in a changing world.

Roy L. Honeycutt

||| 1 |||

A Theology of Social Change

by John M. Lewis

In its simplest terms theology is a systematic, rational exposition of our knowledge of God's nature and purpose. It draws on all sources from which such knowledge may be derived—the created order, philosophy, the great drama of human history, Christian tradition, and especially, the biblical witness to the special revelation of God.

The biblical witness centers on God's relationship to humankind. Theology, therefore, lays great stress on the human situation. As a revelation of the divine nature and purpose, the Bible is also a disclosure of the nature of humanity and our place in the divine purpose. At the heart of theology is the exposition of the divine/human encounter as set forth in the biblical record.

Christian faith affirms that God's revelation reached its fulfillment in the life, death, and resurrection of Jesus Christ. The gospel is the good news that God has provided in Jesus Christ the redeeming love and grace of God for all humankind. Salvation has to do with the gift of a regenerated life that makes us into new persons who are then to live in obedience to the divine will. The gospel, therefore, includes an ethical dimension, without which it is incomplete. This ethical dimension has both individual as well as social aspects.

While the gospel is intensively personal, it is not private. One of the startlingly clear truths of the Bible is that God is not interested in us only as individuals. Our proper relationship to others is central to the entire biblical story of creation and redemption. God is concerned always with the whole human race and all the relational structures by which human life is organized and lived. All human affairs and institutions come under His sovereignty and judgment. Societal structures have their place in the divine purpose, and as such have a specific bearing on the whole question of salvation.

The Bible takes seriously the impact of sin and evil in societal relationships as well as in personal life. Salvation centers in the divine process of reconciliation. Estrangement is overcome; and right relationships are restored between persons and God and between individuals. For God's redemptive purpose to be realized in reconciling persons to one another, whatever exists in society—whether customs, laws, accepted mores, institutional structures, or the misuse of power—that has caused broken relationships and estrangement must be challenged, opposed, and changed.

The redemptive power of the gospel is concerned about all social relationships. The gospel calls us to oppose all that harms our neighbor and to work for those conditions in society that will enable him to fulfill God's purpose for his life. Such commitment calls us to be "agents for social change" as we live in obedience to the divine will as we understand it.

That much in society needs changing there can be no doubt. Is there a theological justification for seeking those changes? Is there anything in our understanding of God's nature and purpose that provides wisdom, guidance, and direction in working for social improvement? Much in every way. This essay will deal with a selection of particular biblical passages and their implications as a theological justification for seeking changes in social relationships and responsibilities that advance the divine purpose. These changes are a fulfillment of our Lord's admonition in the model prayer wherein we are to pray, "Thy kingdom come. Thy will be done *in earth*, as it is in heaven" (Matt. 6:10, author's italics).

Exposition of the gospel has always stressed the need for ethical obedience as a necessary expression of the redeemed life. The major stress for centuries centered on the salvation of the individual, who lives in a world (cosmos) dominated by the "evil One." Tension and conflict between the world, the church, and the believer has been a recurring theme in theology and the ethical requirements of the gospel.

Throughout Christian history various "solutions" have been proposed to the tension between "Christ and culture," no one of which has been universally accepted, though each has attempted to express the sovereign lordship of Christ. The enduring problem is "the conviction that Christ as living Lord" provides the redemptive answer to the human situation on both a personal and social level.[1]

Richard Niebuhr distinguishes the five "solutions" which have found expression in the course of the Christian history, each with its particular "theological justification." A brief description follows, illustrative of the perennial problem facing believers as they seek to be in the world but not part of it, yet accept responsibility as "change agents" to move the world closer to the fulfillment of the divine purpose.

Christ Against Culture exalts the absolute lordship of Christ over all of life, wherein culture can make no ultimate demands on the believer since culture is under the power of the Evil One. The admonition to the Christian is, "Do not love the world or the things in the world. If any one loves the world, love of the Father is not in him"(1 John 1:15, RSV). For the sake of one's personal salvation one must keep oneself separated from the evil world.

The Christ of Culture, declining to see the world as totally and absolutely evil, seeks to harmonize certain "good" elements of society with the Christian faith. The church is not to be totally separated from the world. Accommodation to the so-called "good" elements of society provides a method for a more adequate witness to the gospel. Certain "good" elements of society correspond to the unique moral values of the faith.

Christ Above Culture sees the main issue of life as the relationship and conflict between mankind and God. Christ and the world is not the central issue. However, culture is also the realm in which God's grace operates since its societal structures are ordained of God for the good of humankind. Culture is therefore the context in which the Christians express obedience to God. While the issue of salvation begins and centers in one's relationship to God in Christ in a dimension "above" and apart from culture, a necessary synthesis exists between one's obedience to God in both realms.

Christ and Culture in Paradox takes more seriously the radical nature of sin, which infects all human situations, and is adequately dealt with only by the grace of God. Culture, though thoroughly saturated by sin, is also the realm of God's grace. Culture, even as individual life, is characterized both by sin and grace. Law and grace, divine mercy, and wrath characterize the human situation.

Christ the Transformer of Culture expresses a view that is "more positive and hopeful."[2] Human culture is accepted as a continuation of what God began in creation; sin is the perversion of the good, pervading all human life; and the present world, despite its corruption, is the object of God's redeeming grace and so capable of being changed for the better. Special emphasis is placed on God's active presence in the world, and a person's calling is to be a colaborer with God in fulfilling the divine purpose.

Representatives of the above views can be found throughout Christian history and remind us of the variety of approaches for coming to grips with our responsibility for social change. Such a reminder should prevent us from assuming that *the* Christian solution to all our social problems exists.

Seeing through a glass darkly and knowing only in part, the various approaches make their contributions as we continue to grow in grace, knowledge, and obedience. So it is with the topic of this chapter, "A Theology of Social Change." Here is no claim to present an absolute theological basis for ethical responsibility for social change.

Before looking at some specific passages of Scripture, here is a brief statement of my personal conviction that we have a divine mandate to become "agents of social change" as an expression of our obedience to God.

The lordship of Christ relates to every area of our lives. No part of life can be ruled off-limits to God. Christianity is not a way of living in a certain area of our lives, but a certain way of living in every area of our lives.

Christlike love is the guiding principle by which we live. Made in the image of God who is love means we are made in the image of love. By nature we cannot help loving. The question is, do we love aright?

As a social creature, to be a person means to be related to other persons. God wants life to be shared in social relationships—for us to care for one another. Therefore, we are to oppose all forces that militate against peaceful and constructive social relationships.

Human personality is of ultimate value, both by right of creation and the redemptive death of Christ for every person. Persons are never to be exploited, degraded, misused, or treated as objects. God is always on the side of the oppressed.

As members of society we have a responsibility for the laws, customs, mores, and attitudes that shape and govern our social relationships and structures.

Good works, while never the *means* of salvation, are a necessary and required expression of the life undergoing redemption. They reveal the depth of the likeness of Christ in our lives and our obedience to Christ's lordship.

The reality of sin in social structures, customs, and laws must be taken as seriously as sin in individual lives. It is always more difficult to combat evil in its social forms than it is on an individual basis.

Our citation of biblical passages will not only set forth the biblical basis for these suppositions but will suggest their application to specific problems we currently face in society.

In the unfolding drama of revelation recorded in Scripture, the character and purpose of God are progressively clarified in the Old Testament reaching their heights in the ethical monotheism proclaimed by the great prophets of Israel with the final and complete revelation coming in Jesus Christ.

It is not without special significance that Israel's history was set down in the universal history of the whole human race. The Bible does not say, "God created the Hebrews in God's image," but He created all mankind in His image. And more distinctly yet, male and female were created equally in His image (Gen. 1:26-27; 5:1-2).

The creation narratives have profound implications for our understanding of human nature; mankind's place in the divine plan; and our relationship to and responsibility for each other in society. God is Lord of creation. Humans come under His sovereignty and purpose, and as the crown of His creation, they are special recipients of God's care and compassion. Persons are ends in themselves and are of ultimate value. This truth becomes clear in the New Testament revelation that "God so loved the world, that he gave his only begotten Son" (John 3:16) for the redemption of all mankind.

In the eyes of God every person is of equal worth, no one is to be shut off from His redeeming grace. Jesus loved and associated with all sorts of people; Peter discovered that he was to call no man unclean (Acts 10:15).

Jesus' declaration that "the sabbath was made for man" (Mark 2:27) reflects the ethical principle that social institutions are not ends within themselves. Their worth must be measured in terms of their service to humanity as they express and protect the ultimate worth and dignity of human personality.

The creation narratives also reveal true human nature in God's image. Endowed with capacities superior to all other living creatures, humans are to be colaborers with God in completing His purpose in creation. Bearing God's likeness, they share in God's lordship over nature. Humans are given responsibility for caring for the earth in the fulfillment of the divine purpose. In the command "to subdue the earth" (Gen. 1:28, author's translation), given to both man and woman, a theological mandate is given for scientific research, and man's stewardship of nature is made plain.

Acid rain, environmental pollution, disposal of nuclear waste, the greenhouse effect, protection of endangered species, and protection of the great rain forests of the earth are a few examples of the kinds of problems with which we must deal to fulfill such a responsibility. Acting on these problems means changing society.

The divine intention set forth in the creation narratives, may be summarized: Man is made for *Communion*—a life lived in right relationship to God; man is made for *Conquest*—"to subdue the earth" as its steward; and man is made for *Community*—"it is not good that the man should be alone"(Gen. 2:18), we are to live in right relationship with one another, "we are our brother's (and sister's!) keeper."

The chief concern of God throughout Scripture is to redeem His children because in the wrongful exercise of their freedom, His children thwarted the divine plan. They broke the right relationships of life (to people and nature) and introduced greed, exploitation, prejudice, war, self-righteousness, and the desecration of life and nature into the world.

As holy, righteous, just, and merciful, God's character is the basis of human morality. The image of God in man reflects the moral nature of God. So the Ten Commandments set forth the two basic relationships of life—our relationship to God (the first four Commandments) and our relationship to others (the last six Commandments).

God's concern for righteousness and justice, and for the oppressed and outcast are constant themes throughout the Old Testament. The humane laws of Deuteronomy admonish Israel to care for the needy and helpless, the poor and oppressed, even the stranger within her gates. One cannot miss the concern of God in Scripture—He is not only interested in us as individuals but always in terms of our social and community relationships. It is interesting to observe that the biblical story of redemption moves from man in a garden to man living in a redeemed society—the New Jerusalem.

In His covenant relationship with Israel God reveals His concern for man in community as He seeks to make Israel a light to the nations (Isa. 49:6). Under a new covenant a new community of faith is ordained to carry God's saving message to all the world.

While choosing Israel as His special instrument of revelation and redemption, God is concerned for the entire human race. His moral requirements apply to all nations as He makes plain in Amos's condemnation of Israel's cruel neighbors, but He reserves more harsh judgment on Israel because of her special knowledge (Amos 1:3 to 2:16).

Israel is reminded over and over again of God's concern for all the nations of the earth. "Are ye not as children of the Ethiopians unto me, O children of Israel? saith the Lord. Have not I brought up Israel out of the land of Egypt? and the Philistines from Caphtor, and the Syrians from Kir?" (Amos 9:7) But Israel did not always catch the divine vision, as evidenced in Jonah's rebellion against God's missionary concern for Nineveh.

Israel's prophets constantly reminded the nation that moral obedience to God's will was more important than the correct observance of religious ritual (Micah 6:6-7; Amos 5:21-24). The requirement of moral obedience is most succinctly summarized by Micah: "He hath showed thee, O man, what is good; and what the Lord doth require of thee, but to do justly, and to love mercy, and to walk humbly with thy God?" (Micah 6:8)

The ultimate foundation of Christian theology is the revelation of God's character and purpose in Jesus Christ (Heb. 1:1-3; Col. 1:15, 19; 2:9). God's love, as expressed in the deeds and teachings of Christ, sets forth the pattern and power of our guiding principle for ordering personal and societal relationships and responsibilities (John 15:11).

The way Jesus treated others reflects the ultimate worth of human personality. He associated with all sorts of people, from all walks of life, and gave special attention to the oppressed and those who were rejected by society. He repeatedly broke through social, economic, and religious customs that erected barriers between persons.

Many of His parables—like the lost sheep and lost coin; the good Samaritan; the prodigal son; and the rich man and the beggar at his gate—deal with the ultimate worth of persons, God's concern for them, and our obligation to care about one another.

As the incarnation of God's redeeming love, the life of Jesus Christ, therefore, is the "theological basis" for Christian obedience. In Him God shows us how to live, how to treat one another, and how to apply the gospel to all areas of life.

God's revelation in Christ provides for the restoration of the divine image (Col. 3:10; Rom. 8:29; 1 Cor. 15:49). The God of Creation is the One who completes His purpose for us in Jesus Christ. "For God, who commanded the light to shine out of darkness, hath shined in our hearts, to give the light of the knowledge of the glory of God in the face of Jesus Christ" (2 Cor. 4:6).

From its beginning the church has sought to minister to the less fortunate: to care for widows and orphans, the poor, the sick and suffering. The industrial revolution brought a ground swell of changes in society in time to shock the church awake to apply the social implications of the gospel to the growing problems of urban life.[3]

Following the War Between the States, a rising crescendo of voices within the church sought to "mobilize" and stir the moral conscience of Christians. Many volunteer organizations arose to deal with the growing problems brought on particularly by the industrial revolution: alcoholism and its effects on family life, and society in general; poverty, slums, the labor movement. Abolition societies and the temperance movement were among the most notable of such volunteer organizations.

The formation of so many volunteer organizations in this period of our history shows that to be effective in bringing about social change, concerned and committed Christians must join together in many forms of concerted action. Further evidence is the fact that every major denomination has in its own way "organized" for social action, though all too often the church has lagged behind groups outside the church which have led the way in taking courageous stands to combat the evils of society.

As the church carries on its traditional ministries to those wounded and hurt by the evils of society, in obedience to the gospel it must move into the arena of "preventive ministry," combating and seeking to eliminate those forces that bring on the hurt in the first place.

The social application of the gospel became a central and major concern for the American church following the War Between the

States, as the church faced the impact[4] of the industrial revolution and scientific thought on society. While the social implications of the gospel were recognized from the beginning, it was not until the latter half of the nineteenth century that serious efforts were made to apply the gospel fully to the problems of society. Known as the "social gospel movement," this attempt to bring the gospel to bear on society's ills became one of America's distinctive contributions to an understanding of the Christian faith.[5]

The early decades of the twentieth century witnessed the formative period of the social gospel movement, most clearly articulated by Walter Rauschenbusch, often called the "Father of the Social Gospel." His incisive and proactive writings—such as: *Christianity and the Social Crisis* (1906); *Christianizing the Social Order* (1912); *The Social Teachings of Jesus* (1916); and *A Theology of the Social Gospel* (1917)—joined a host of other books, pamphlets, journals, and teaching aids calling for the application of the gospel to the ills of society. In all its various expressions, although often misunderstood and maligned by its detractors, the social gospel made a dynamic, necessary, and lasting impact on modern Christianity.

For Rauschenbusch "the ultimate value of human life, the solidarity of the human family and the necessity for the strong to 'stand up for the weak'!"[6] were clear directives for applying the gospel to the social problems of the day. Jesus' teaching about the presence of the kingdom already in the world is to be taken with utter seriousness and its three laws of service, sacrifice, and love[7] obeyed as the dynamics releasing a redemptive force in society.

Rauschenbusch never forsook his evangelical roots nor failed to emphasize the continuing necessity for the salvation of the individual. Nor did he ever propose the "social gospel" as a substitute means for such a personal experience of saving faith. What he did insist upon was that the follower of Jesus has a moral responsibility to apply the gospel to the social issues of life.

Jesus was not looked upon as a social reformer, but the source of the ideals and moral principles by which society is to be judged and reshaped. Obedience to the ethical demands of the Sermon on the Mount is the necessary expression of the redeemed life, having both a personal and social application.

For the Christian, the life and teachings of Jesus, therefore, become the theological basis and justification for involvement in social change. To be so committed arises out of the awareness that much in society militates against the will of God, degenerates human personality, and thwarts the fulfillment of the divine purpose in creation.

The commitment also arises out of the awareness that as one of God's servants each one of us is called to become "salt, light, and leaven." The necessity for social change presupposes that the structures and dynamics that make society what it presently is—mores, customs, laws, life-styles need changing. Since society is made up of people, social change ultimately means changing people. The first and basic concern of the gospel, therefore, is the redemption and conversion of persons. But the gospel cannot stop there.

Nor is it sufficient merely to turn "redeemed individuals" loose, one by one, to serve as "salt, light, and leaven." Joint action and organized group power are also needed. Each has its place to fill in applying a theology for social change.

Following the example of Jesus, the individual believer can demonstrate in personal relationships the *agape* kind of love learned from Jesus. One can, like Jesus, break the taboos and "cross the line" of social customs that demean and degrade human beings, as Jesus did in talking with the woman of questionable character at the well in a culture when men did not even talk with their own wives in public! One can express acceptance of the essential equality of women as Jesus did in teaching Mary the Torah in public in a culture where men thought it necessary to burn the Torah rather than let a woman touch it, much less study it!

The ultimate goal of social change is to produce a more just society. In its simplest terms, justice is seeing that "each man gets his due," as Justinian reminded the Romans long ago. From a theological point of view, justice is seeing that each one has the right to become what God intended in the creation for persons created in His image. "God has willed that we be God's free, fulfilled creation reaching our highest goals. The highest goals of the human community are found in the sharing love of God as expressed in the compassionate ministry and the redemptive suffering of God's Son, Jesus Christ."[8] Any element of society that hinders, or makes more difficult the attainment of that goal for any individual, is a target for social change.

A just and righteous society has been God's expressed concern throughout Scripture, for which the Ten Commandments were given as guiding principles. While religious observances in ritual and sacrifice were acceptable expressions of one's right relationship to God as set forth in the first four Commandments, such rituals, according to the prophets, were always secondary to God's requirement that obedience to the second table of the law, man's relationship to his fellow-man, must reflect the moral character of God in the life of the worshiper. Isaiah makes the case most clearly. In chapter 1:11-15, he pronounces severe judgment on "mere religiosity," concluding his diatribe in verses 16 and 17 with God's clarion call: "Wash you, make you clean; put away the evil of your doings from before mine eyes; cease to do evil; Learn to do well; seek judgment [justice and righteousness], relieve the oppressed, judge the fatherless, plead for the widow."

Amos made the same case, in chapter 5, verses 21 to 23, ending with God's requirement, "let judgment [justice] run down as waters, and righteousness as a mighty stream."

Jesus made the same case against the self-righteousness of the Pharisees so careful to observe religious ritual while omitting "the weightier matters of the law, judgment, mercy, and faith" (Matt. 23:23).

In His description of the last judgment in Matthew 25, Jesus made treatment of the neighbor in loving and just ways a central criterion for determining our obedience to God and the revelation of how extensively His love must come to permeate our own being.

Jesus' description of His own ministry in Luke 4 becomes an exemplary pattern for our involvement with the neighbor, and a theological basis for seeking social change. His example of servanthood calls us to follow in His train. His call to take up our own cross requires us to emulate His sacrificial love in all life's relationships and responsibilities. His insistence that His kind of loving become the hallmark of the true and faithful follower, finding expressing in its dual obedience to love God with all our being and our neighbor as ourselves, becomes evidence that God's image has truly been restored in us.

Out of the realistic awareness that "we have here no abiding city," that only God will complete the perfect kingdom "beyond history," that the "wheat and tares will grow together," and that sin and grace coexist in both the individual and society at large, as Luther reminded us, one may well ask, "What then is the use in seeking social change, since no work of man abides nor can it be the means of salvation?"

William Hendricks has stated the case succinctly, "A theological basis for Christian social ministries is the same as a theological basis for all our relationships to God—grateful obedience."[9] One basis for social change is that God has required it—"He hath showed thee, O man what is good; and what the Lord doth require of thee, but to do justly and to love mercy, and to walk humbly with thy God" (Mic. 6:8).

Another element in a theological basis for social change is its relationship to the evangelistic imperative of the gospel. To help the hurt and needy, to champion basic human rights, to help shape society so it enhances everyone's right to a full, peaceful, and meaningful existence, may be more proof of our love for the neighbor we are seeking to win to a faith in Christ, than empty words that, in the face of human hurt and need, seem to "pass by on the other side." Brooks Hays states this aspect of the case most pointedly, "Christians must be busy reordering society through sound and appropriate political action. We must be building an environment in which justice prevails and which makes victory in the Christian struggle more likely."[10]

Article XV of *The Baptist Faith and Message* is a provocative statement of a theological basis for social change:

Every Christian is under obligation to seek to make the will of Christ supreme in his own life and in human society. Means and methods used for the improvement of society and the establishment of righteousness among men can be truly and permanently helpful only when they are rooted in the regeneration of the individual by the saving grace of God in Christ Jesus. The Christian should oppose in the spirit of Christ every form of greed, selfishness, and vice. He should work to provide for the orphaned, the needy, the aged, the helpless, and the sick. Every Christian should seek to bring industry, government, and society as a whole under the sway of the principles of righteousness, truth and brotherly love. In order to promote these ends Christians should be ready to work with all men of good will in any good cause, always careful to act in the spirit of love without compromising their loyalty to Christ and His truth.

Notes

1. Richard Niebuhr, *Christ and Culture* (New York: Harper and Row, 1951), 2.

2. Ibid., 191.

3. Bill J. Leonard, "The Modern Church and Social Action," *Review and Expositor* (Spring 1988): 243-253. The paragraphs that follow draw heavily from Leonard's incisive article.

4. Charles Howard Hopkins, *The Rise of the Social Gospel in American Protestantism, 1865-1915* (New Haven: Yale University Press, 1940), 208.

5. Ibid.

6. Hopkins, 208.

7. Ibid.

8. William L. Hendricks, "A Theological Basis for Christian Ministries," *Review and Expositor* (Spring 1988): 221.

9. Ibid., 221.

10. Brooks Hays, *Home Missions*, July-August 1974.

||| 2 |||

The Minister as Proactive Agent of Change

by Larry L. McSwain

Every minister is an agent of change. The rapids of change swirl around the church as they flow with new intensity.[1] One can navigate against the current, harness its power for useful purposes, or be swept along in its path without resistance. Every minister has a choice in the face of change—react to it by seeking shelter from it, work to enhance the *status quo*, be swept along without direction, or work for specific goals and objectives in the face of it.

This chapter advocates the need for all of these responses, depending on the issues and circumstances being faced. Most ministers, however, never practice the option of deliberate leadership to accomplish specific changes which would not have occurred without such leadership. Roland Warren defines two kinds of change in his analysis of social change. The first of these he calls *crescive change* which he defines the "kind of change that is occurring 'out there' independent of our own change efforts."[2] If one believes change is crescive nothing is done in the face of it. It is assumed that there is an inevitable direction of history which cannot be altered by human action.

The other view of change, which Warren advocates, is what he calls *purposive change*. He says, "When we talk about purposive or deliberate or planned change, we usually mean 1) a process deliberately undertaken to achieve some objective, 2) considered from the viewpoint of the individual or group seeking the change objective."[3] This is what is meant by "proactive change." It is deliberate planning in order to effect the outcome of a group, church, community or larger social system. This chapter will explore dimensions of proactive change on the part of ministers.

G. Willis Bennett has given thirty years of his life teaching ministers to be proactive agents of change. His emphasis is both thoughtful and practical. He believes ministers ought to study the change process and from that study apply the gospel to real-life church and community settings. Drawing from the wisdom of my mentor and friend, I have set forth the essential roles of the minister as a proactive agent of change. Each is important and all are needed in the course of the change process. Some persons are more gifted than others for particular roles. However, significant change will require participation in all of the following roles at some particular level.

The Change Agent as Theorist

Theory implies to some an "ivory tower" view of reality and suggests a detached uninvolvement in the real world. Yet, every change must have a thoughtful perspective if it is to be accomplished. This is what I mean by theory—the application of specific knowledge in guiding a decision or change. The most effective theory of change is multi-disciplinary. It integrates insights from a variety of areas of understanding.

The first discipline necessary for a change theorist is theological conviction. Change derives from a particular view of God's activity in the world. The proactive change agent believes in the transforming power of the gospel. As Jesus came preaching the kingdom of God, (Mark 1:14) He set forth a standard for the transformation of the world. Telling and doing the kingdom of God is the task of the change agent. Like Jesus, the change agent proclaims the power of God from beyond human history. The kingdom of God must invade our lives and our structures. When it does, change occurs.

Jesus set forth His own agenda for change in His inaugural sermon in Luke 4:16-18. Change was to embody the spirit of God in human experience. When such occurs, human life becomes different. The blind see. The poor are fed. The downtrodden are freed. Good news is proclaimed and salvation is experienced.

The apostle Paul summarized the impact of the gospel in human experience. "Therefore, if anyone is in Christ, he [or she] is a new creation; the old has gone, the new has come" (2 Cor. 5:17, NIV). A theology of change is an essential aspect of an adequate theory of the change process. This is what makes the minister unique among agents of change. It is not that we do not utilize the best insights of the social sciences. Every human understanding of change is needed. But we must recognize that lasting change, righteous change, is transcendent in quality.[4]

The second discipline necessary for a proactive change agent is sociological awareness. One must have an understanding of changes occurring within the larger society and within one's immediate context of ministry. It should be clear to those who are older that profound changes have altered the way churches do their work of ministry.

When one compares the 1990s with the 1950s, several significant trends affecting the church can be observed. It is my judgment that ministry is more difficult now. That is not because people are less committed, but because there is less cultural support for doing ministry now. One's sociological awareness needs to include both the broad social trends affecting ministry as well as local situations. First, there is a persistent religiosity in the culture. Levels of belief within the American society are still very high in comparison to earlier periods of time. Those beliefs remain high, however, only so long as they are broadly defined. For instance, nine out of ten Americans say they believe in God. That does not mean, however, they are willing to practice any institutional expression of that belief in a local congregation.[5]

The second trend is a redefinition of institutional loyalties. There has been a general loss of confidence in institutions in our society, including government, educational institutions, business corporations, and the church. Because of this there is a lessening of commitment to participation in local churches while high levels of belief continue.

The third major trend is a shattering of traditional moral values.

While many traditional values remain intact, those related to sexual practices, the roles of women in society and the home, and family values have changed drastically.[6]

The fourth observable trend is a weakening of denominational loyalty. Lines have blurred between denominations as a result of intermarriage and switching among the major denominations. There are also fewer social and educational differences between denominational groups. No longer must one change denominations as a way of achieving social status. Denominations hold more positive attitudes toward one another than in the past.

A fifth trend of which change agents need to be aware is the growth and power of Roman Catholicism. Roman Catholics have outgrown Protestants in every region of the United Sates and rapidly so in the South and West. This has brought an increased religious polarism within the nation. Most of the larger cities of the country are predominantly Roman Catholic in religious preference.

The emergence of a strong tension between liberals and conservatives is a sixth trend. Recent polls indicate that 43 percent of the American public claims to be religiously liberal, 41 percent religiously conservative, and 16 percent are unable to say.[7] The mobilization of right-wing movements and reactions against the growing liberalism of the 1960s resulted in a growth of conservative churches and conservative beliefs.

A seventh trend is the pluralization of religious choices. Some of the faster growing small groups in American society come from religions that are non-Christian and outside the context of the United States. Asian sects, cult groups, and Islam are growing rapidly within this country. Along with these movements we have seen the rise of parachurch movements which have served to create more choices for religious expression.

An accompanying aspect of this pluralization is the growing ethnic character of our population. Between 500,000 and 600,000 immigrants arrive in the United States annually. Most of these are from Hispanic or Asian nations. Current estimates are that by 2000 there will be 8 million Asians, 25-30 million Hispanics, and 34-36 million blacks in the United States.

The rise of the Pentecostal and charismatic movements constitutes still another trend. Since the Azuza Street revival in Los Angeles in 1906, which gave the Pentecostal movement national attention, there has been a rapid increase in Pentecostalism. That has resulted in the growth of both Pentecostal denominations and the charismatic movement within existing denominations.

One of the newer trends is the emergence of therapy as a form of religious expression. Many self-help, holistic health, psychological helping approaches have assumed a near status of religious commitment among highly educated groups. This gives rise to a strong sense of individualism in place of the community commitments of Christian faith. While many churches have provided ministries of care and psychological support which are valuable, secular forms of therapy have replaced participation in the congregation for significant segments of American people.

In sum, one could say the final trend is a restructuring of American religion. Our religious environment is quite different today from thirty or forty years ago. The tensions now are between liberals and conservatives within the same denominations. Each of those groups often has more in common with other denominational groups that have similar viewpoints. A dominant influence from Roman Catholics and conservative Protestants along with the loss of institutional viability for some congregations of almost every denomination can be observed. The rise of the megachurch is proving to be the most important congregational change to alter this trend.

In addition to these broad social trends, the change agent needs to be aware of local community change. Shifts in population growth, an understanding of the sources of population growth or loss, a clear picture of racial and economic change, alterations in the age structure of the population, and a host of other demographic variables are important in strategies of change. The change agent who leads people to act without a clear understanding of the social context in which that action in being planned is an irresponsible agent.

The third discipline in our multidisciplinary theory involves psychological insight. The change agent needs to understand the impact of change on individuals and how group dynamics can be utilized to motivate and encourage persons to act. The change agent also needs to be well aware of the sources and products of anger which can be a significant driving force in change. One must decide whether anger produces negative or positive changes. Generally speaking, anger seldom works as an effective motivation for long-term change in the church or the community.

The Change Agent as Analyst

The second fundamental role of an effective proactive change agent is analysis of the change objectives to be accomplished, the target of such change, sources of resistance to the change, how one may mobilize a group to accomplish change, the choice of a particular strategy of change, and decisions regarding the institutionalization of change after it is accomplished.[9] Effective change requires the skills of analyzing the setting in which change is to be accomplished. I have already given attention to the sociological factors which need analysis.

Another aspect of analysis includes the power structure one faces in affecting change. Change occurs in the context of structure. Every congregation has a power structure whether informal or formal, and every change in a congregation must deal with that structure. Understanding how power works, that power agents can be resisters or promoters of change, and perceptions of approaches that will lower the resistance of power to change are all important skills.

A third step for analysis is a study of needs for ministry. Whenever one collects information about the levels of poverty, inadequate housing, substandard incomes, disabilities, abuse, violence, or other areas of concern, consciousness is raised as a basis for change. Information can be a powerful ally in effecting change.

Finally, the change agent needs to be a good evaluator. Effective change requires an evaluation of what has happened. Ministers with the skill of examining how well programs work are invaluable. Much of the change needed in the church is the elimination of activities which do not accomplish meaningful goals.

The Change Agent as Strategist

A third important role for the proactive agent of change is to plan specific approaches to achieving one's objectives. There are two general guidelines for change strategies. The first of these is to "choose what is possible." A proactive change agent is not a Don Quixote jousting with windmills. Many persons get caught up in causes, ideas, or issues which are impossible to address given the resources of the change agent and the disposition of those with whom the agent works. Agents of change ought to focus their energies in realistic directions.

This does not mean that there is no room for pursuing the ideal. Ideals drive our willingness to engage in changing the possible. The individual, however, who is always pushing for changes that lack support frustrates coworkers and usually ends up in a loss of energy called "burnout."

A second principle is "choose what is right." The Christian change agent must have a commitment to those changes which embody the vision of God's kingdom. We are more than simply practitioners of social processes. We are moral agents of change. There must be a driving ethical consciousness behind all change efforts if they are truly to be called *ministries* of change.

There are five strategies which can be employed in the change process. The first of these is the *exertion of power*. Many attempt to achieve change by organizing a political process and attempting to impose change on all who would resist. Many of the decisions of the church resemble more the character of a political convention than open processes of decision making. Robert Dale calls the leader who uses power as the basis of leadership the commander.[10] Others would prefer the word *dictator*. Such approaches to change can be effective, and there are circumstances in which exerting power may be the only means for accomplishing a needed change. Power strategies seldom generate lasting change unless they are enforced with new rules, however. Such a strategy is most appropriate for crisis situations or settings in which the change is being driven by a clear moral imperative.

A second strategy for accomplishing change is *compromise.* The negotiator is also a role proactive change agents may need to assume. Negotiation works best in a situation where there is some balance of power, and the only means of achieving change is to bargain for an agreement between competing parties or loyalties. Both sides must gain something and lose something if compromise is to be effective. While compromise is never the ideal, it may be a necessary strategy in ministry. The skills of bargaining are needed by effective agents of proactive change.

A third strategy for accomplishing change is to offer personal *support.* Pastors have learned that by encouraging individual members of a congregation and developing warm and caring relationships, advice is heeded when leadership is offered. One pastor-friend I know describes his relationship with a state legislator who is not a member of his church. During their frequent visits, the legislator often discusses difficult decisions he has to make. As a result of this caring relationship, the man trusts the advice of his pastor-friend. Change has come as a consequence of these pastoral conversations with a powerful figure. Dale calls such a leadership style as encourager.[11] The encourager gives personal support and provides help to others in times of need. Out of this trusting relationship a change occurs.

A fourth strategy is *withdrawal.* Dale calls this kind of leader the hermit.[12] The hermit is one who decides that the best course is inactivity. While many would consider such a style not to be a style for change leadership, in reality it is. When the minister chooses not to address an issue, the outcome of that issue is determined by silence. A poster of the 1960s which circulated among many young people quoted Harvey Cox "not to decide is to decide."

The last strategy for change is to become a *catalyst,*[13] of win-win processes. One form of proactive change is to lead persons of like-minded values to work together. Persons who do this facilitate healthy processes where people come together and collaborate on their vision for the future, establish goals and directions for that future and work in harmony toward their accomplishment. While this is an ideal style of change leadership for the church, it requires an environment with a high degree of trust between those working together, patience on the part of the leader and skill in group processes and decision making.

The most important skill for a proactive change agent is to know which of these strategies is needed for a particular situation. In reality, one might employ every strategy just described. There are times when the best strategy for change is to wait silently for a more opportune time to move forward. On some occasions collaboration is possible. There are situations in which the best mode of leadership is to engage an evil situation with power that overwhelms the evil with good. Compromise may be needed in a host of situations, else the best is lost as a result of inflexibility on the part of those who desire change.

The Change Agent as Actor

The ultimate aim of the ministry of change is action. Theory, analysis, and strategy are prelude to the heart of the matter. When the minister bears witness to another of the truth of the gospel the change of evangelism comes. Leading the congregation to study its community and engage in new social ministries is the action that bears fruit of change. Writing letters to Congress, voting, and lobbying for new legislation are the actions of political change.

The Book of James is the text of the true change agent. It is laced with appeals for Christian action.

> Be doers of the word, and not hearers only (1:22).
> Religion that is pure and undefiled before God and the Father is this: to visit the orphans and widows in their affliction, and to keep oneself unstained from the world (1:27).
> If you really fulfill the royal law, according to the scripture, "You shall love your neighbor as yourself," you do well (2:8).
> So faith by itself, if it has no works, is dead (2:17).
> Whoever knows what is right to do and fails to do it, for him it is sin

(4:17).

Perhaps action is difficult because we lack the courage of Jesus. He was the greatest agent of change the world has known. He transformed life. When He preached the kingdom of God, lives were set on a new direction of commitment to that kingdom. They were never the same again. When He taught parables of a new way of living, persons were confronted with new insights for daily living. We still experience transformation when we live by these teachings. Jesus healed and brought forth the experience of grace in the lives of hurting people. His people are called to continue the ministry of healing to a hurting humanity. Jesus challenged the structures of the Temple and resisted the control of the state over His life. Those actions cost Him His life. But in sacrificing Himself, He showed the power of God over every human evil and the promise of transfiguration for the future. The Christian doctrine of the resurrection is the promise to every agent of change that the way of truth will ultimately triumph over every form of sin, evil, and injustice in the world. Thus, the proactive agent of change must follow the way of the cross in self-denial and in trust that the pain of change will bring forth new life. Without the promise of resurrection, the courage of proactive action will be difficult to muster.

The Change Agent as Priest

The proactive change process is not completed until the attempts at change have been accepted by those who were the targets of change. Many changes have been attempted which were temporarily received but once the change agent was removed from the situation, the group reverted to its former values and behavior. It takes prophetic action to mobilize human beings into new behaviors. It takes priests to nurture and build a nest around those changes so they will last.

The priest is essentially an institutional builder of changes inaugurated by prophetic action. Seldom can the person who leads the change process be the priest who builds consensus around such change. However, it is possible. Different styles of leadership are required to institutionalize priestly change from those required to inaugurate prophetic change.

The priest is a builder of consensus. The priest must have an open relationship with all those who have been through the change process. Priests listen. Priests support. Priests attempt to smooth hurt feelings. Priests work for the participation and the expression of feeling by all those who have been affected by change.

A second role of the priest is that of process guide. A priest must be skilled in those aspects of decision making which cause people to move together in their decision-making processes. Every proactive agent of change needs to have partners capable of leading those who are attempting change to move together with healthy processes. Once a target of change has encountered those attempting the change, processes of rebuilding trust and maintaining the victories won are essential.

Finally, the priest is a developer of rituals which remember accomplished changes. Change is maintained by celebrating in worship the changes accomplished. Whenever a new ministry has been inaugurated in the life of a congregation, worship needs to celebrate the successes of that ministry. Whenever the alteration of a constitution has resulted in new rules for the guidance of a congregation, rituals of remembering those new directions are required. Whenever new persons have experienced the transformation of life in confession of faith in Christ and baptism as His follower, rituals of remembrance will reinforce the commitment of individuals to their new faith. This is why there should be no contradiction between a community which worships the Lord Jesus Christ and a community which follows the prophetic actions of the Lord Jesus Christ. New changes call for new rituals and new forms of worship.

Change agents also need to understand the role of priests as resisters to change. Often the greatest difficulty of a proactive change agent is confronting one's own brothers and sisters who have institutionalized established patterns in resistance to the new. Underestimating the power of priestly religion can deter effective change. Sometimes the truest prophet is the minister who learns how to be a more effective priest to those who would resist change.

The Change Agent as Opponent of Change

One of the most unexplored arenas of change agentry is opposition to change.[14] The true discerner of God's righteousness and justice will perceive that many changes are to be opposed. A proactive agent of change is not always working for a new direction, but sometimes resisting a new direction. My colleague Anne Davis has posted on the door of her office Gandhi's famous statement "Non-cooperation with evil is as much a duty as is cooperation with good." The church has a role of maintaining the good along with bringing forth the good. Sometimes the most effective agent of change is that hardheaded, tough-skinned individual who simply stands against the new. Whenever change brings forth less concern for hurting persons, less than a full vision of Jesus' teaching and preaching of the kingdom of God, and less than a commitment to the truth of Scripture, it should be opposed.

Notes

1. Robert Theobald, *The Rapids of Change: Social Entrepreneurship in Turbulent Times* (Indianapolis: Knowledge Systems, Inc., 1987).

2. Roland L. Warren, *Social Change and Human Purpose* (Chicago: Rand McNally College Publishing Company, 1977), 9.

3. Ibid., 12.

4. See Larry L. McSwain, "Foundations for a Ministry of Community Transformation," *Review and Expositor* 77 (Spring 1980): 253-272, for a further development of the importance of a theology of changes.

5. These trends are summarized from a number of sources including Jackson W. Carroll, Douglas W. Johnson and Martin E. Marty, *Religion in America, 1950-1978* (San Francisco: Harper & Row Publishers, 1979); Lyle E. Schaller, *It's a Different World* (Nashville: Abingdon Press, 1987); Wade Clark Roof and William McKinney, *American Mainline Religion: Its Changing Stages and Future* (New Brunswick:Rutgers University Press, 1987); and Robert Wuthnow, *The Restructuring of American Religion:*

Society and Faith Since World War II (Princeton: Princeton University Press, 1988).

6. I have described several of these changes in "The Committed Christian in a Modern Society," *Witnessing Giving Life* (Nashville: SBC Stewardship Commission, 1988), 177-192. Daniel Yankelovich, *New Rules: Searching for Self-Fulfillment in a World Turned Upside Down* (New York: Random House, 1981) is a primary source for research on value changes.

7. Wuthnow, *Restructuring*, 133.

8. The estimates are from U.S. Bureau of the Census projections and estimates of *American Demographics* magazine.

9. These are the essential elements of Warren's model of social change. Cf. *Social Change and Human Purpose.*

10. Robert D. Dale, *Ministers As Leaders* (Nashville: Broadman Press, 1984), 21-23.

11. Ibid., 23-24.

12. Ibid., 24-25.

13. Ibid., 18-21.

14. Lyle E. Schaller, *The Change Agent: The Strategy of Innovative Leadership* (Nashville: Abingdon Press, 1972), 140ff., develops the idea of the use of power in resistance to change.

||| 3 |||

Preaching and Social Change

by C. Welton Gaddy

In the fall of 1968, in a one-on-one graduate reading seminar, G. Willis Bennett outlined for me a course of study relating the ministry of the local church pastor to the dynamics of social change. To be answered immediately was the question of whether or not any positive relationship—any direct relationship—between pastoral ministry and social transformation could be documented. Pursuit of an informed response to that inquiry necessitated a careful consideration of both theory—homiletical and sociological—and history—secular and ecclesiastical.

Well aware that the reasons for and contributors to social change are always multiple and diverse, I wanted to know about the significance of religion generally, the place of the church specifically, and the role of a pastor even more particularly in this process. As a matter of fact, my interest was even more narrowly focused. I brought to my study a long-held interest in preaching which found expression in a bias toward the pulpit as a source of power within both the church and society. I well recall the excitement of beginning an inquiry into materials which could either validate my hunch about the importance of homiletics or mandate a complete reassessment of the worth of this part of a minister's work. That enthusiastic interest continues to this day and undergirds the words here offered in honor of one who has challenged, encouraged, enlightened, and affirmed this pastor-preacher.

Definitions

Debates continue regarding the relationship or the lack of a relationship between preaching and social change. Most students of preaching point to a social dimension of Christian proclamation which yields an interpretation of issues and a call to responsible action. However, devotees of social analysis seldom acknowledge the role of the pulpit in social processes. Sociologists of religion and church historians are most likely to document only the fact that reciprocal influences are exchanged between religious institutions and social institutions. Thus, the interests of the church—liturgy, preaching, education, and ministry—interact with the dynamics of society—movements, institutions, reforms, issues, and problems.

Prior to any further reflection regarding either preaching or social change, each of these two important terms needs to be defined. Informed interest in this discussion requires a common understanding of its major components.

Preaching

A classic description of preaching came from an 1877 series of lectures on preaching by Phillips Brooks at Yale. This highly regarded rector of Trinity Church in Boston declared that real preaching is "truth through Personality."[1] For several years I was satisfied with Brooks's definitive phrase. However, with the passing of time spent in studying preaching, other church ministries, and society, I decided that no dimension of Christian proclamation could be taken for granted. I wanted the specifics spelled out.

Three factors are involved in Christian preaching: (1) the intention of God, which is the will of God or the word of God (one part of what Brooks referred to as "truth"); (2) the human medium, which is the preacher (Brooks's "personality"); and (3) the contemporary situation, which involves both personal and social concerns (the other part of Brooks's "truth," the realm in which and to which the will of God is applied). Thus, for me, an expanded and more detailed form of

Brooks' definition is in order. Preaching is God revealing through human proclamation His intention for persons in both their private and social relationships. Apparent immediately is the potential for the preaching ministry to affect society.

Social Change

Similar to the task of identifying so many other concepts and terms in sociology, defining social change is an exercise which must not overlook the obvious. The words *social* and *change* are understood experientially even if the thoughts involved are not articulated theoretically. *Change* describes documentable differences in anything which occur over a period of time. *Social* refers to the realm of interpersonal relationships. Thus, "social change is a continuous process over a period of time in which differences in human relationships take place."[2]

Agreement on a definition of social change is much easier than consensus regarding the primary causes of social change. Some writers prefer to explain social change by means of predictable, influential social processes—cooperation, competition, conflict, accommodation, and assimilation.[3] However, certain more specific factors are incontrovertible—biology, technology, environment, cultural values. Certainly the importance of individuals must be considered. A renowned thinker such as Thomas Carlyle attributed all positive social change to great persons.[4] At this point the potential impact of religion becomes most noticeable. Sociologists recognize that individual attitudes toward social issues are influenced directly by the spirit which pervades the organization and functions of religious groups.[5]

Easily verifiable is the interaction which takes place between religious change and social change. Most students of sociology relate this interaction to one of three categories—religious change which results from social change, religion as a hindrance to social change, and religion as an initiator of social change.[6] What is true in the broad category of religion generally is also applicable to the narrow concern of preaching specifically. Preaching is shaped by social change even as preaching shapes social change.

Reflections: Preaching as a Social Act

Not only is preaching a theological, ethical, and liturgical act, preaching is a social act. Recently, Arthur Van Seters stated the truth succinctly, "Every sermon is uttered by *socialized* beings to a *social* entity in a specific, *social* context and always at a *social* moment."[7] Several years ago Jitsuo Morikawa pointed to the same homiletical reality when he described preaching as "a public proclamation of a public deed that has public meaning and repercussion."[8] In the preaching event both the medium and the message are social. Preaching is a social act. A careful consideration of the context and content of Christian preaching can increase one's appreciation for the importance of this fact.

Social Context

Social context is an influential factor which must be considered in selecting the biblical text which gives rise to a sermon, the decision of the preacher about the style and language to employ in the delivery of a sermon, the preoccupations of the congregation which affect their hearing of the subject matter in a sermon, and the applications of the truth of a sermon made by the preacher and members of the congregation. Social factors such as political loyalties, economic status, and family stability directly impact preaching—its interpretation of Scripture, its formation in the church, and its application to the world—as well as receive attention from preaching. Unquestionably, society influences preaching and preaching influences society.

Nowhere is the significant impact of social context on the preaching task any better demonstrated than in the preacher's treatment of a biblical text. In the first place, each passage of Scripture chosen for sermonic treatment was formed in a specific social context. Though outside the scope of this essay, that is worthy of recognition.

Second, the effective preacher must anticipate how the congregation will hear a specific text. Here social context is decisive. People listen to the message of the Bible through "sensitivities that may distort, emphasize, enhance, or censor."[9] Often the text heard may be very different from the text read.

Robert McAfee Brown has made a valuable contribution to persons who read the Bible within the social context with which we are familiar in the relatively affluent United States.[10] Brown argues forcefully that persons who study the Scriptures from a vantage point of privilege and comfort do not hear the same message that is heard by Third World Christians who listen to the Bible amid oppression and poverty. Biased by our social context we may even screen out passages of Scripture that call into question our values and threaten our lifestyles. Such is the case with both preachers and listeners.

Third, between the formation of a text in the ancient past and the reception of that text by a contemporary congregation stands the interpretation of that text in the preaching event. In a sense, preaching is not so much "an act of reporting on an old text but . . . an act of making a new text visible and available."[11] At this point, preaching turns from being a recipient of the influence of the social context to functioning as a contributor to the social context. The strategy of preaching is to use biblical texts either to legitimate the present social situation or to present a life-world that causes a crisis by offering a challenge to the present and posing an alternative.[12]

Interpretation is a primary function in both the social context of preaching and the act of preaching itself. Sociology charts society restructuring itself. Central in this process is interpretation—reflecting on ancient memories and traditions while recasting those memories and traditions in new ways which resonate with a new situation.[13] The potential power of preaching, an interpretive act in itself, is clear. Walter Brueggemann addressed this very point and concluded, "The key hermeneutical event in contemporary interpretation is the event of preaching . . . preaching is such a crucial event not only in the life of the church, but in our society."[14]

Within any given social context preaching presents a credible way of life that can be appropriated, a way of life by which people in a society are authorized and permitted to embrace a different way of life. In this regard, two tendencies within our society are fundamentally unacceptable to preachers—a false kind of objectivity which assumes the world is closed, incapable of change, and a kind of subjectivity which posits that people are able to conjure up private worlds with no sense of accountability to or infringement from the larger public world.[15] The task of preaching is to revitalize people's religious imagination so as to create a sense of open space which gives people enough hope to work for social change.[16]

The social context in which preaching occurs affects even the form, language, and style of sermons effective enough to influence social change. Language, properly used, actually can help to determine social attitudes, behavior, roles, and structures. When aware of the social function of language, preaching "can use language in such a way as to encourage social effects that are appropriate to the gospel."[17]

In his *Theopoetic* Amos Wilder observed that human nature and human societies are more motivated by images and visions than by ideas.[18] Both sociologists and homileticians are aware of this truth. Preaching which significantly impacts society must challenge the metaphors which dominate its social context with images of faith.[19] To take aim at social change requires preaching which enters the realm of the heart. Of course, rational, discussive, and programmatic content cannot be ignored in such preaching, but evocative, metaphorical, and well-near poetic content is essential.

In summary, a study of the social context in which preaching takes place reinforces the accuracy of the description of preaching as a social act and documents the powerful reciprocal dynamics extant between preaching and society. In the preaching moment sociological realities interact with biblical-theological truths. The work of the person in the pulpit identifies that preacher as a product of the present society. At the same time, the preaching which emanates from that pulpit presents a worldview, elaborates a gospel, and endorses a moral climate which shape the very fabric of society.[20]

Bifocal Content

Several years ago James Cleland coined the term "bifocal preaching" in reaction to the "homiletical heresy" of "monofocality."[21] Based upon a careful study of the preaching patterns in the Bible, a theological understanding of the Word of God, and an informed perception of the social creatures in any given congregation, Cleland concluded that effective preaching must speak to both the good news (the gospel) and the contemporary situation (which obviously includes society). To ignore either focus in the preaching event is to err.

When preaching centers on the biblical materials alone, it may be interesting, informative, and even inspirational but it is not likely to be relevant. Listeners are left with a firm grasp of God's truth about Jerusalem, Antioch, or Corinth but with no real help regarding the meaning of God's truth where they live. Conversely, when preaching pays attention only to the contemporary situation, it may prove to be accurate in its analysis, informative in its suggestions, and relevant in its spirit but devoid of the much-needed promise of redemption—silent rather than declaring a redemptive word.

Thomas Troeger was right when he wrote that "The most radical voice for social change in the pulpit is not the one that sounds like the editorial page of the evening paper or a television commentator. Instead, it is the voice whose analytical speech draws fire from the visionary energies of depth language and (like the biblical prophets) shakes the foundations of the state with poetic thunder."[22]

The sermon is birthed out of dialogue between the message of the Bible and the issues which make up the contemporary situation. Preaching may begin at either place—in the Bible or where people are. However, regardless with which it begins, preaching must move to the other. Christian preaching affirms the truth which erupts when the world of the Bible and the world of today collide. Don Wadlow posits that it is in the communion of these two "social worlds the word of God speaks meaning to people and even becomes the chemistry of change in that people."[23]

In some instances preaching may overtly endorse one particular social program over another or explicitly recommend a certain course of social action. However, the presence of structural details, organizational agendas, and partisan political agendas in preaching should be the exception rather than the rule. Extreme reticence is in order when pondering the possibility of speaking for or speaking against a named personality within a sermon. Much more appropriate, not to mention mandatory, is a sermon's attention to the principles, prejudices, and attitudes which yield social effects. Preaching has spoken to critical social issues in every generation of faith.

Great preaching in any age does not ignore the significant issues of that age. Stated another way, authoritative preaching will give attention to communities as well as churches, taxes as well as tithes, metropolitan planning policies as well as evangelical missions needs, strategies for social organizations as well as agendas for pastoral ministries, voting as well as witnessing, welfare as well as worship.[24] One highly respected student of preaching spoke to this matter forcefully, "Preaching is authenticated by the extent to which the social dimension is taken into account."[25]

Preaching which brings into proper relationship the Word of God and the words of people, the world of the Bible and contemporary societies, eternal truths and temporal concerns, is what Cleland called the "homiletical corollary of the doctrine of the Incarnation." Each sermon is a contemporary Incarnation with "its head in the heavens but its feet . . . on the ground."[26] Such preaching is a social act which contributes to social change.

Observations: the Power of Preaching in Society

In the early spring of 1968, I was a part of a group, made up mostly of Southern Baptists, which gathered in the White House Rose Garden to hear some remarks from the President of the United States. Tension permeated the nation. Racial integration within the nation was proceeding against a threatening, sometimes-violent opposition. The somewhat-beleaguered President made an impassioned plea to the preachers and other religious leaders present requesting their assistance in promoting the cause of social justice. Not only did President Lyndon Johnson know the importance of the religious publications and programs produced by a denominational bureaucracy, he recognized the power of the Christian pulpit in touching the hearts, altering the attitudes, and supporting the principles which could result in meaningful social change. What President Johnson recognized during his turbulent administration was a truth which has been documented in almost every generation—the power of preaching in society.

Old Testament prophets declared the word of God related to the most pressing issues of their societies. No subject was off-limits. Prophets challenged injustices of all kinds and called for the establishment of social righteousness. Changes within society were often accompanied by a rough treatment of the catalysts for change—the prophets—but changes did occur.

The great tradition of proclamation in the Old Testament reached even higher peaks of power in influence in the New Testament. Ponder the number of positive social changes precipitated by the life and preaching of Jesus—care for prisoners and provisions of food for the hungry, a refutation of violence and initiatives for peace, respect for children and freedom for women, provisions for poor persons and justice in economic systems, to name only a few. In numerous instances decades and even centuries have passed before the seeds of social righteousness planted by the preaching of Jesus have broken through the crusty soil of society and blossomed for all to see. Some very potent truths from the Master Preacher still await a full realization within our culture.

History documents the power of preaching in society. Consider the role of the pulpit in the American experiment. More than one person has pointed to the profound influence of preaching during the immigration and settlement of this land.[27] Pioneers looked to preachers for guidance in the face of family crises, Indian attacks, epidemics, and civil strife. In fact, the American pulpit became the sounding board for discussions of the individual's role in society.[28]

Many historians recognize that the preachers in the colonies were as responsible as the politicians for kindling and fanning the flames of the American Revolution. "Independence" was the subject of many sermons in the churches as well as the topic of numerous orations in political forums. Church pulpits became posts of great power. Preaching laid a theological foundation for the Revolution and sounded both a personal and national challenge for participation in it.

During America's "dark night of the soul" preaching persisted as a powerful force in society though its aim was often the maintenance of an evil status quo rather than a challenge to the morally abominable institution of slavery. Vested interests helped to determine the content of sermons. One survey of this period described how "ministers found their proof texts and interpreted Scripture to make it seem to approve slavery for the planters while condemning it for the abolitionists."[29] By the time the Civil War began, antagonistic—in fact, directly contradictory—sectional positions had been affirmed in preaching as the truth of God.

To be sure, some preachers did rise above prevailing social currents to help shape new forces. Theodore Parker and Henry Ward Beecher stood out as influential opponents to slavery. Historians indicate that the powerful antislavery preaching of Parker exerted great political influence on prominent figures such as Sumner, Chase, and Lincoln.[30]

At the beginning of the twentieth century significant social reforms were underway and prominent preachers were addressing social issues. The coexistence of those two phenomena was not coincidental. Sensitive preachers were reacting to conditions in society and at the same time attempting to alter those conditions. Preachers such as Walter Rauschenbusch and Washington Gladden left no uncertain sound regarding the gospel's judgment upon and imperatives in relation to immoral social problems. Interestingly, though these two men made a significant impact on the societies in which they lived and permanently altered the posture of mainline Protestantism toward social issues, they viewed themselves as preaching evangelists primarily concerned with the salvation of persons—new evangelists committed to both personal and social evangelism.

In recent years, numerous pulpiteers have exercised the power of the pulpit to initiate, influence, or prohibit social change in their respective parishes and cities. However, one name is preeminent in this regard. Seldom has a preacher singularly touched the heart of an entire nation and contributed so dramatically to major alterations in its social arrangements as did Martin Luther King, Jr. The Civil Rights movement in the United States—its motivation, convictions, methodologies, and resilience—cannot be understood apart from the preaching of this man. Even the most cynical perspective on preaching's power to influence social change is confounded by the wide-ranging repercussions of King's ministry.

Speaking on the high priority of the pulpit ministry in one specific congregation, a preacher stretched the breadth of his vision and concluded, "Preaching is God's chosen means of redeeming, transforming, and reshaping human history."[31] Sociological evidence from a study of our society corroborates that theological assertion.

Directions: An Opportunity and a Challenge

Preaching has taken its lumps in recent years. Some people are convinced that preaching can hardly keep a congregation awake much less move a society to change. For whatever reason—a loss of the church's influential status in society, a preoccupation with visual rather than audible communication media, impatience with speaking vis a vis acting—preaching has fallen out of favor with many thoughtful people.

Unfortunately a great deal of preaching is dull, boring, and irrelevant. Preachers prattle worn-out platitudes in an unnatural voice and an unfamiliar vocabulary. Texts are lifted from the pages of the Bible with no consideration for the social context in which they were formed and attached to pet pulpit topics which appear to have no significance for the personal and social lives of the listeners. Some preaching ought to be out of favor in the human community.

But, not all preaching! Problems do exist with specific preachers and certain congregations. However, preaching rightly done remains one of God's greatest gifts to the church for the betterment of persons and societies. Authentic preaching continues to exert the kind of power which can positively effect social change.

What kind of preaching can effect social change? What is authentic preaching? Remember the definition with which this chapter began. Then, consider the following qualities of such preaching.

Biblically Based

Christian preaching must take seriously the Holy Scriptures. Church pulpits exist to declare the gospel. As social concerns—political, economic, familial—relate to the biblical message, they become appropriate subjects for inclusion in the contents of sermons. However, preaching on socially related themes must retain a homiletical integrity and not be reduced to sociological essays. The Word of God is central. If a preacher has no more to say on a subject than that which has already been communicated via newsprint or the electronic media, the matter should be left alone. Justification for preaching on social concerns is directly related to the convictions formed by biblical truths.

Theologically Sound

Social agendas ordered by sermon topics should be consistent with basic theological beliefs—the sovereignty of God, the purpose of creation, the nature of persons, the character of love, the fact of sin, the certainty of judgment, the necessity of redemption, the priority of grace. Preaching about social action—analyses, plans, and recommendations—which is not deeply rooted in theological truth is likely to be incapable of withstanding the heat generated by tough questions, harsh criticisms, and special-interest group's opposition. Congregational responses to socially oriented proclamation should have the benefit of insights regarding the spirit, style, and methods of action consistent with faith.

Sociologically Realistic

I once saw a comparison of two social studies conducted among members and pastors of the same churches. The pastors were asked to list the three most prevalent problems of families in their congregations. Then, members of the congregation were requested to name the three most frequently recurring problems in their families. When the two lists were set side-by-side, they were completely different—not one single issue was held in common. Obviously, the preaching of those pastors was addressing nonissues for their members and failing to offer help for their people's greatest needs.

Generalizations out of touch with realities, recommendations ignorant of actual possibilities, and convictions which have taken no account of the costs of helpful actions do not belong in authentic preaching. The stakes are too high. The pulpit is an intersection where biblical-theological truths and sociological realities meet.

Effectively Delivered

Persuasive preaching requires some evidence of the preacher's passion concerning the sermon's object of attention. Just because a given sermon is carefully reasoned in its assertions, development, structure, and style, that does not mean the preaching of that sermon must be devoid of emotion. Listeners are quick to detect a situation in which the words spoken do not seem to come from cherished convictions. Preaching which impacts social change appeals to the head and heart, to reason and emotions.

Actionally Supported

Preachers noted for their contributions to social change often find opportunity for many types of service to society. Orations from the pulpit are only one part of a larger ministry which might include membership in service organizations, participation in city council or school board meetings, writing articles for journals and editorials for newspapers, and speaking in secular settings, as well as faithfulness in traditional pastoral duties. Often the credibility for what is declared in the pulpit is established by the activities of the preacher in the institutions and movements of society.

Repeatedly Willis Bennett raised the question, "How can we be unconcerned about anything for which God is concerned?" That inquiry is rhetorical but not theoretical. Just as sociology and religion interact influentially, so do preaching and social change. With that knowledge, the conclusion of this chapter consists of a much-needed confession of preachers and a highly desirable aspiration regarding the position and conviction of their hearers. The words are from a Salvadoran peasant mass: "We truly believe that God's word has come to us and made us change."[32]

Notes

1. Phillips Brooks, *On Preaching* (New York: The Seabury Press, 1964), 8.

2. Everett M. Rogers, *Social Change in Rural Society* (New York: Appleton-Century-Crofts, Inc., 1960), 4.

3. Lyle E. Schaller, *Community Organization: Conflict and Reconciliation* (New York: Abingdon Press, 1966), 36.

4. Kelly Miller Smith, *Social Crisis Preaching: The Lyman Beecher Lectures 1983* (Macon, Ga.: Mercer University Press, 1984), 51.

5. Joachim Wach, *Sociology of Religion* (Chicago: The University of Chicago Press, 1962), 49.

6. J. Milton Yinger, *Religion, Society, and the Individual* (New York: The Macmillan Co., 1965), 266.

7. Arthur Van Seters, "Introduction: Widening Our Vision," *Preaching as a Social Act: Theology & Practice*, ed. Arthur Van Seters (Nashville: Abingdon Press, 1988), 17.

8. Jitsuo Morikawa, "Public Proclamation," *The Riverside Preachers*, ed. Paul H. Sherry (New York: The Pilgrim Press, 1978), 13.

9. Walter Brueggemann, "The Social Nature of the Biblical Text for Preaching," *Preaching as a Social Act*, 128.

10. Robert McAfee Brown, *Unexpected News: Reading the Bible with Third World Eyes* (Philadelphia: The Westminster Press, 1984).

11. Brueggemann, 128.

12. Ibid., 147.

13. Ibid., 135.

14. Ibid., 138.

15. Ibid., 147.

16. Thomas H. Troeger, "The Social Power of Myth as a Key to Preaching on Social Issues," *Preaching as a Social Act*, 213.

17. Ronald J. Allen, "The Social Function of Language in Preaching," *Preaching as a Social Act*, 168.

18. John H. Westerhoff III and John D. Eusden, *The Spiritual Life: Learning East and West* (New York: The Seabury Press, 1982), 45.

19. Troeger, 208.

20. Allen, 173, and Paul D. Simmons, "The Minister as 'Change-Agent' "*Review and Expositor*, 68 (Summer 1971): 364.

21. James T. Cleland, *Preaching to Be Understood* (Nashville: Abingdon Press, 1965), 33-55.

22. Troeger, 223.

23. Don M. Wardlaw, "Preaching as the Interface of Two Social Worlds: The Congregation as Corporate Agent in the Act of Preaching," *Preaching as a Social Act*, 80.

24. C. Welton Gaddy, *Proclaim Liberty* (Nashville: Broadman Press, 1975), 72-73.

25. Smith, 13.

26. Cleland, 45, 57.

27. Harold A. Bosley, "The Role of Preaching in American History," *Preaching in American History: Selected Issues in The American Pulpit, 1630-1967*, ed. DeWitte Holland (Nashville: Abingdon Press, 1969), 26, and DeWitte Holland, "Sermons in American History: An Introduction," *Sermons in American History: Selected Issues in the American Pulpit, 1630-1967 (Na*shville: Abingdon Press, 1971), 15.

28. Raymond Bailey, "Building Men for Citizenship," *Preaching in American History: Selected Issues in the American Pulpit, 1630-1967*, ed. DeWitte Holland (Nashville: Abingdon Press, 1969), 135-36.

29. Holland, 18.

30. Smith, 53.

31. Morikawa, 11.

32. Justo L. Gonzalez and Catherine G. Gonzalez, "The Larger Context," *Preaching as a Social Act*, 40.

||| 4 |||

Evangelism in a Changing Social Context

by Roy E. Godwin

In a world that convulses with the throes of change, Christianity marches to a divine drumbeat. Often it charges; sometimes it retreats. It cannot stand still. Its goal is the consummation of God's kingdom, its marching orders are Christ's commission, its message is the good news of peace, and its hope is that all will be saved.

The world does not wait passively for the church to accomplish its tasks of enlisting faithful converts, training them for loving service, and then changing society for the better. It seems that the world marches to its own drumbeat of change, good and bad. The church may lead at times while at other times it lags behind, but absent it is not.

However we may describe the church in this changing world, we must admit that it faces a tremendous challenge in every aspect of its being and ministry, particularly in evangelism. This chapter explores the challenge that social change presents to church evangelism and suggests some ways the church may respond.

The Art of Evangelism

A place to begin is with a clear understanding of what evangelism is. The term has been defined in a variety of ways, ranging from simple definitions such as "It is everything that the church does to communicate the gospel to the world," to rather elaborate, more comprehensive definitions. Delos Miles provides a most commendable definition.

> Evangelism is being, doing, and telling the gospel of the Kingdom of God, in order that by the power of the Holy Spirit persons and structures may be converted to the lordship of Jesus Christ.[1]

Similarly another definition that offers clarity and breadth as well as direction for action is used by the American Baptist Churches, U.S.A. It appears in their Policy Statement and serves as a guide for their evangelism programming.

> Evangelism is the joyous witness of the People of God to the redeeming love of God urging all to repent and to be reconciled to God and each other through faith in Jesus Christ who lived, died, and was raised from the dead, so that being made new and empowered by the Holy Spirit, believers are incorporated as disciples into the church for worship, fellowship, nurture, and engagement in God's mission of evangelization and liberation within society and creation, signifying the Kingdom which is present and yet to come.

Both definitions are theologically sound and practical. They put the gospel into proper relationship to Jesus Christ, the kingdom of God and the church. Another aspect that is especially commendable is their emphasis upon the work of the Holy Spirit in evangelism, for evangelism certainly must be of the Spirit if it is to work. No matter how sound our sociological analysis, theological basis, or our methods may be, without the Holy Spirit as the agent of evangelism, our efforts will be futile.[2]

Another step would be toward the rich metaphorical definitions of evangelism by D. T. Niles in his book, *That They May Have Life*. One familiar definition is "It is one beggar telling another beggar where to get food."[3] Granted, that line is lifted from a larger context that develops further the concept of proclamation and service in evangelism, but it goes beyond the literal words to a greater, more profound truth and moves us toward the art of evangelism.

In this age there is an increasing interest and respect for that which is spiritual even in the midst of advancing technology and the strong influence of secular humanism. The Gallup organization, for instance, found in a recent research study, *The Unchurched American*, that a majority of Americans are religious even though many do not choose to affiliate with a local church or synagogue. To reach people, evangelism should be seen as the art of communicating the good news of God's rule through Jesus Christ under the power of the Holy Spirit so that faithful persons and structures of society may be joyously redeemed.

The substance of this definition is basically the same as the others, but the emphasis upon evangelism as an art is different. There is a tendency to reduce evangelism to a science in which formulas and steps are memorized and revival events are carefully programmed and institutionalized. According to this definition the witness practices the art of communication like an artist translates a vision onto a canvas so graphically that one who sees it is moved from the depths of being so that there is the joyous response of spirit to Spirit. There is such insight that one can no longer be the same as before. One is drawn to be a part of all that is true and good and beautiful, inspired by that Beatific Vision behind that which is upon the canvas.

Or again, the witness is a player upon a stage who so catches the Spirit of the Writer that the actor is transformed and embodies that spirit within the role. The audience responds to the powerful movement inspired within their own souls in wonder and awe. They are caught up in the divine drama, themselves acting out with the one on stage the unfolding of the joyous life so as to be transformed into a new, higher life-style with eternal dimensions. The actor embodies the truth in character and plays the role with depth and freedom so as to adapt to mood and circumstance. There is no one way to *play* the role when the actor *is* the role.

This definition is an attempt to resist the confines of exact predetermined and memorized words and to move to a depth of being that responds under the influence of the Holy Spirit with integrity and emotion toward the person and/or social structure in need of redemption. It attempts to combine being and doing with telling. Also it fits with the concept of Christianity as a movement rather than only an institution.

A final point in our definition is the role of the church. George F. Sweazey reminds us that the church is the evangelist. "The evangelist is not a person at all, but a fellowship. God put His church on earth as His intended instrument for evangelism." It is a normal activity for all the church people all the time.[4]

It should be clear by now that the issue is not whether or not to evangelize. Rather it is a given, considering what lies behind it and considering the nature of the church. Furthermore the task is everyone's—the church as a whole and in part, including pastors, professional evangelists, other professional ministers, and laypersons.

As the church intentionally sets out to accomplish its evangelistic task it would do well to recognize that it is a divine-human institution within a social context. As such, it should know its theological basis for evangelism which includes its own nature, its understanding of God as Creator, Sustainer, Redeemer, and Lord, the nature of humanity and sin, the meaning of the incarnation and salvation. The church also needs a clear understanding of its message for the world.

Along with that theological basis, on the human side there ought to be a sociopsychological awareness of the context. In that regard dialogue with the sciences which give insight into people and circumstances is indispensable. Such insight helps understand the dynamics of social change and its effect upon people and structures of society. Personal change such as the crises within human development as well as social change affecting people and institutions provide ongoing opportunities for ministry and evangelism if the church has a proper attitude toward change.[5]

The study of history provides indispensable insight into church's response to its context and judge its success within that interplay. For example, three of the four national spiritual awakenings had profound social implications as the church initiated and encouraged change toward social reform.[6]

One may conclude that every Christian's privileged task is evangelism—artfully communicating the good news of Jesus Christ in the power of the Holy Spirit to all of society that all who faithfully respond may be redeemed. To accomplish this task the church must confront the tremendous challenge of a continually changing social context.

The Challenge of Social Change

As other chapters of this volume will attest, social change presents a formidable challenge to the Christian church, and not only to the church but to other social institutions as well. The church is caught up in a vast array of demographic and ecological changes in society and among its own constituency and structure.[7] The most outstanding of these shifts include urbanization and other population shifts, immigration and attending pluralism, advances in technology, and increases of both affluence and poverty.

Furthermore it should be recognized that changes may come as readily from the disintegration of counterpressures as well as from those efforts by persons and institutions acting out their societal roles. It may be argued that change induces change.[8] The church is no exception to this process as it proclaims a gospel with change at its heart—conversion. Also its ministry is an intentional activity to change persons and circumstances for the good—redemption. Its nurturing, worshiping fellowship causes Christian growth—sanctification. Who would deny the connection between any one of these roles with evangelism?

The changing social context presents the church with challenge and exciting opportunity. The challenge is complex and many-faceted. It both activates and creates concern; it causes doubt and fear while offering hope and opportunity. The church cannot avoid the powerful forces of change, but must respond intentionally to determine a viable future for itself. To choose otherwise would run the risk of becoming irrelevant and dying.[9]

What is said of social institutions and business corporations regarding response to changing society may be said of the church as well.

Tom Peters, coauthor of books on the virtues of excellence in business, calls for a redefinition of excellence. He suggests that excellent firms do not believe in excellence, only in constant improvement and constant change. "Excellent firms of tomorrow will cherish impermanence—and thrive on chaos."[10] It would not take much imagination to translate those terms into religious language.

Accepting the givenness of change, a wise church seeks continuity within change.[11] It must discern what is permanent and everlasting and what is transient and changing about its message to an everchanging world. Another word from Tom Peters: "If you are not reconfiguring your organization to become a fast-changing, high-value-adding creator of niche markets, you are simply out of step."[12]

Toward More Effective Evangelism
in a Changing Society

Given the magnitude and force of change, it is amazing that the church does as well as it does, not only to cope but to thrive. One must admit that our successes are surely of the Spirit and not our doing. That does not dismiss us from trying to be wise as serpents while being harmless as doves. Therefore let us briefly examine some of the methods and means used by the church in its evangelistic ministry.

The church constantly strives to discover new methods and devise new means in order to meet the challenges of the changing social context. While one would be intrigued with the seeming plethora of ways to evangelize that are being used by churches today, George A. Sweazey claims that modern methods are not new. He reduces them to ten: "sermons, classes, friendship, partnership in humane tasks, home contacts, conversations, church fellowship, intimate groups, the arts, and the communication media." What is needed is an updating of these so as "to be more contemporary than the morning paper in its vocabulary and its adaptation to modern ways of thought and living."[13] The purpose of this chapter is not to provide a listing and critique of specific methods and means used in evangelism. What is proposed is that one move beyond these to principles that may guide the church toward greater flexibility and effectiveness.

The variety of approaches used in personal evangelism has been reduced by some writers to two basic methods: deductive and inductive. Delos Miles, seemingly leaning more toward the inductive, has provided a helpful summary of both approaches and offers an approach that blends the two.[14]

The deductive method begins with the general and moves to the particular, while the inductive moves from the particular to the general. Some characteristics of the deductive approach include greater responsiveness by those whose receptivity is high, monological style—telling the message (often perceived as memorized and delivered by rote), proclamation and confrontation, and highly rational method. The inductive approach begins with the prospect whose receptivity may be low and presents the message through dialogue with emphasis upon affirming the prospects and listening to their needs. It produces long-term results because it is spontaneous, relational, and incarnational.

The deductive approach is used largely in Evangelism Explosion training, Campus Crusade's Lay Institutes for Evangelism, and in the Lay Evangelism Schools, and Continuing Witness Training of Southern Baptists. Proponents of the inductive approach include Ralph Neighbor's "Target-Group Evangelism" and George G. Hunter. The latter has adapted effectively this approach to Abraham Maslow's hierarchy of human needs.[15]

Miles presents a combination model following the FORM anagram (family, occupation, religion, message) as a technique to guide conversation intentionally from small talk to presentation of the gospel. Such a technique is helpful as long as it includes a careful understanding of the prospect and allows for a response by the witness under the leadership of the Holy Spirit. It is commendable for its balance of intentionality and genuine concern for the person so as to recognize both physical and spiritual need and speak to both.

Another area challenged by social change is the use of mass evangelistic events such as revivals and crusades. Under the leadership of

Charles Finney in the nineteenth century, American revivalism shifted its focus from frontier camp meetings to urban church revivals. The popularity of these revivals brought opposition from some of the more educated clergy, especially in the Northeast. Such opposition still exists and is compounded by the changing life-style of the urban dweller. However, revival meetings continue to be popular as an evangelistic method and a social cultural event. This is often true among ethnic groups who settle in the large cities of America.

A hypothesis that bears testing is that as evangelistic methods such as revivals become institutionalized, following the pattern described by Ernst Troelsch as a transition from sect-type to church-type, the methods become less effective in evangelism. It appears that with institutional development, church growth tends to occur as much or more so through transfer of membership than through additions by conversion.

However, if mass evangelism is less effective than personal evangelism, nevertheless it is effective in some sectors and among some people. The degree to which it is effective should give instruction for its rank among the priorities of churches and denominations in their evangelistic ministry. Again proper balance is called for.

Continuing the theme of balance, another area of concern in evangelism is its relationship to social action and social ministry. Our definition includes a concern for the redemption of social structures and social institutions, including the family. One has simply to ask "For what area or aspect of life does God not care?" Can God's people do less?

As Christ is our supreme model of evangelism, we note that He balanced the Great Commission with the Great Commandment. He saw our neighbor as neither a bodiless soul nor a soulless body nor even a body-soul isolated from society. Following His example, Christians must be concerned for the total welfare of their neighbor as body-soul-in-community.[17]

Christ balanced love of God with love of neighbor and love of self. Further He balanced love for God equally through heart, soul, mind, and strength (Matt. 22:37; Mark 12:29). Again, He balanced healing of the spiritual problem along with the physical problem (Mark 2). Likewise Christians are to balance love for persons with love for causes as we reach out in ministry to persons' needs and in action to set right the forces of injustice. With such balance the church may proclaim its message with integrity. Truly as Ken Chafin has said, "Evangelism moves forward best on the wings of ministry."[18] Through ministry and social action the church affects change rather than simply responding to the forces of change that affect it and people outside the church.

Social change affects evangelism with individuals. Rapid change may cause one to open up to new possibilities as values are challenged, hopes dashed, and truths shattered. When that which one has trusted has been lost there is a tendency to explore other possibilities. Evidence of such has been found in foreign nations who experience defeat in war or by foreign persons transported to a new land with a new dominant religion.

The transitions that occur in human development provide occasions for consideration of the gospel. One would do well to explore the literature dealing with those personal transitions to determine the ultimate questions of life that arise in transition times and determine how the good news of Christ answers those questions. Persons may be most open and responsive in these times.[19] Such changes occur from time to time, and so a person who is closed to the gospel today may be receptive later.

There seems to be a built-in resistance to change in every person. People tend to resist change in their personal lives, especially if they are satisfied with their condition. This may be due to a perceived threat to one's free choice and one's freedom of behavior. Yet it seems that one's primary anxiety is due to a hunger for a cause which would give purpose to one's life. Knowing that these and other psychological issues are churned up by change, the witness would do well to become familiar with the approach advocated by George Hunter mentioned earlier which pays close attention to Maslow's hierarchy of needs.[20]

Three New Approaches

Though Sweazey maintains that there are no new methods in evangelism, only old ones being improved, let us look at some contemporary approaches. The first means of evangelism that is experiencing renewed success in sharing the good news is the use of story.

Certainly this is not a new means but rather is the oldest. What is new is an interest and understanding of its structure and power. Like most forms of art it has greater impact than what is immediately apparent. No wonder Jesus used parables and stories as He preached and taught eternal truths.

James O. Stallings has reminded us of the common place of story among all people but especially among black churches in America.[21] Ranging from the narrative account of certain events to the most intimate personal story, truth is passed from one person to another. Whether it is a chronology of bare facts or an imaginative story rich with metaphor, what counts is the truth that is conveyed and the change that occurs within the hearer.

A new dimension of the use of story has to do with story listening. It is one thing to tell a story; it is another to listen for the truth buried within it. John Savage of L.E.A.D. Consultants, Incorporated, has sought to train church visitors in the art of contacting church dropouts, with an emphasis upon listening skills including story listening. Just as one cannot not communicate, one cannot not tell one's story however abstract or clear it might be. Such a skill is most useful in evangelism—to understand the needs of the prospective believer as he tells his story and respond with the appropriate presentation of God's story for that person.

A second means that is proving to be helpful in evangelism and outreach is the use of typological studies. Given the overwhelming numbers of people in our pluralistic urban society any skill that simplifies the process of understanding people can be a valuable tool.

One approach is the use of typology to classify persons in terms of life-style and values. This is not to slight their personhood or identity but rather is an approach to understand persons and their needs. It also helps in designing a strategy of outreach and ministry by the local church or judicatory for its constituency. When one understands who the unchurched persons are—their values and beliefs—one may respond more effectively with ministry and message.[22]

Another use of typology based upon the studies of C. G. Jung, Katherine Briggs, and Isabel Briggs Myers in personality types is helpful in understanding the complexity of human behavior. The Myers-Briggs Type Indicator is used to establish individual preferences and promote more constructive use of the differences between persons. This kind of analysis is not an attempt to categorize people so as to predict their behavior or to assist in attempts to control others. It actually celebrates the wonder of our differences and similarities and promotes greater understanding among persons.[23]

One particular study by Roy M. Oswald and Otto Kroeger, *Personality Type and Religious Leadership*,[24] has been helpful in local churches and denominational judicatories. It has aided churches in identifying the gifts of members and helped leaders plan and execute church ministries with greater patience and understanding.

The third means for evangelism is the art of communication, especially as it is informed by the study of cybernetics. As one practices active listening one relates to another in such a degree of rapport as to set up a cybernetic loop that feeds back to the prospect and enhances the progress of the communication.[25] The relationship tends to bind the parties together in friendship as care and understanding pass between the parties.

This concept has great potential in the witnessing conversation which leads toward conversion. One major concern has been the number of apparent decisions made for Christ that do not seem to last. There is an initial affirmation of belief but no lasting change seems to occur, and in time that person goes back to the old life-style. What would it take to make the decision last?

It may be said that if one is truly converted by the Holy Spirit, that conversion will last. How is the witness to know that the convert will truly have a lasting change of heart and character? Indications may come from the following type of conversation.

The witness who is backed by a Christian life-style and prepared through prayer and knowledge of Scripture begins a conversation with the prospect with the full intention to seek the good for that prospect. Primary emphasis is upon being saved to a new life more than being saved from sin, although the latter is not neglected. The prospect is led to sense what the new life would be like for him/her by projecting through sight, sound, and feelings what that life-style means. The element of time is introduced by exploring when and where the prospect will make a decision. The witness is careful that the decision is initiated and can be maintained by the convert, and that the decision for the new life will preserve that which is good and positive in the life of the prospect. The new convert continues in a caring relationship with the witness beyond this conversation and is introduced into the fellowship of a nurturing congregation.

G. William Schweer has emphasized the importance of the Christian communicator's following through beyond the convert's initial decision. The time immediately after the decision is crucial because of the possibility of dissonance that occurs after major life decisions. The convert needs the help of the witness and the church. The process of discipleship is unending as one is encouraged through worship, nurture, inspiration, and instruction to grow in spiritual maturity.[26]

Conclusion

In summary it may be evident that in the context of social change there is a bias toward principle in comparison with method.[27] As one practices the art of Christian witnessing one would achieve greater flexibility, innovation, adaptability, and experimentation through being guided by principles than by being confined to strict methods. An approach that is built upon principles opens up more choices.

Another important principle of personal evangelism is that of beginning with the prospective convert, receiving what is communicated, and responding to perceived need. This approach combines being an active listener with sensitivity to social and psychological insights that may help determine the way the gospel message is presented for salvation.

Finally, there is a need for balance in our evangelistic efforts from personal witnessing and on through the levels of church, local judicatory, and national denomination.[28] There should be both deductive and inductive approaches, both personal and mass evangelistic efforts, and both personal and public witness. Such balance keeps us true to our calling to seek the salvation of whole persons in the whole world.

Notes

1. Delos Miles, *Introduction to Evangelism* (Nashville: Broadman Press, 1983), 47.

2. Francis M. DuBose, "The Practice of Urban Ministry," *Review and Expositor*, 80 (Fall 1983): 521.

3. D. T. Niles, *That They May Have Life* (New York: Harper and Brothers Publishers, 1951), 96.

4. George E. Sweazey, *The Church as Evangelist* (New York: Harper and Row, Publishers, Inc., 1978), 47f.

5. Roy E. Godwin, "Contemporary Social Change and the Protestant Pastor: Implications for Southern Baptists," (Ph.D. diss., The Southern Baptist Theological Seminary, 1972), 21ff.

6. Samuel Southard, *Pastoral Evangelism* (Atlanta: John Knox Press, 1981), 154f.

7. David O. Moberg, *The Church as a Social Institution*, 2d ed. (Grand Rapids: Baker Book House, 1984), 47f.

8. Thomas C. Cochran, *Social Change in America: The Twentieth Century* (New York: Harper and Row, Publishers, 1972), 53, 93.

9. Joseph S. Zaccaria, *Facing Change* (Minneapolis: Augsburg Publishing House, 1984), 6ff.

10. Tom Peters, *Thriving on Chaos* (New York: Alfred A. Knopf, 1987), 4.

11. Moberg, 513ff.

12. Peters, 53.

13. Sweazey, 47.

14. Miles, 253ff.

15. Ibid.; see George G. Hunter, *The Contagious Congregation: Frontiers in Evangelism and Church Growth* (Nashville: Abingdon, 1979), 39ff.

16. Miles, 235f.; DuBose, 516. See also Bill J. Leonard, "Evangelism and Contemporary American Life," *Review and Expositor* 77 (Fall 1980): 495ff..

17. Delos Miles, *Master Principles of Evangelism* (Nashville: Broadman Press, 1982), 78f.

18. Ibid., 83. For more extensive treatment of this issue see Delos Miles, *Evangelism and Social Involvement* (Nashville: Broadman Press, 1986). See also Leonard, 505; Henry J. Schmidt, ed., *Witness of a Third Way* (Elgin: Brethren Press, 1986).

19. G. William Schweer, *Personal Evangelism for Today* (Nashville: Broadman Press, 1984), 118f. See also Daniel J. Levenson, *The Seasons of a Man's Life* (New York: Alfred A. Knopf, 1979); Gail Sheehy, *Passages* (New York: E. P. Dutton and Co., 1974); William Bridges, *Transitions* (Menlo Park: Addison-Wesley Publishing Co., 1980); Donald McGavran, *Understanding Church Growth* (Grand Rapids: William B. Eerdmans, 1970).

20. Schweer, 41ff, 120. See also Jard DeVille, *The Psychology of Witnessing* (Waco: Word Books, 1980).

21. James O. Stallings, *Telling the Story: Evangelism in Black Churches* (Valley Forge: Judson Press, 1988).

22. See Michael J. Weiss, *The Clustering of America* (New York: Harper and Row, Publishers, 1988); J. Russell Hale, *The Unchurched* (New York: Harper and Row, Publishers, 1980); Robert D. Dale and Delos Miles, *Evangelizing the Hard-To-Reach* (Nashville: Broadman Press, 1986).

23. Otto Kroeger and Janet M. Thuesen, *Type Talk* (New York: Delacorte Press, 1988) and David Keirsey and Marilyn Bates, *Please Understand Me* (Del Mar: Prometheus Nemesis Book Company, 1984).

24. Roy M. Oswald and Otto Kroeger, *Personality Type and Religious Leadership* (Washington: The Alban Institute, Inc., 1988).

25. Paul Watzlawick, Janet Beavin Bavelas, and Don D. Jackson, *Pragmatics of Human Communication* (New York: W. W. Norton and Company), 126f.

26. Schweer, 105f. See also pp. 99ff. for excellent discussion of James Engel's and Ralph Neighbor's Models of receptivity, and George G. Hunter III, *To Spread the Power* (Nashville: Abingdon Press, 1987), 63ff.

27. Miles, *Master Principles of Evangelism*, 4.

28. For a further development of the theme of balance see David O. Moberg, *Wholistic Christianity* (Elgin: Brethren Press, 1985).

||| 5 |||

The Challenge of the Cities
by George W. Bullard, Jr.

Introduction

The cities of the world have challenged every discipline and movement known to mankind. Christianity has found cities to be both the place of its greatest expansion and its greatest frustration.

As the world wrestles with the challenges of the 1990s, the cities will be no less of a challenge than they have been before. In the next generation Christianity will face the possibility of losing ground in many cities, particularly the world-class cities.

From now through approximately the year 2015, the next generation, Christianity also has an opportunity to share the hope found only through Jesus Christ. This chapter addresses twelve challenges which the Christian church faces. It also suggests ways to deal with these challenges.

The focus of the challenges will be upon the United States because of the depth of knowledge this writer has concerning missions work within America. However, many of the principles can be applied to global missions work.

During the next generation the people of America will continue the march to the cities, as they have done since the first United States census in 1790. This march will not be to the central cities, but to the metropolitan areas. Increasing urbanization of the total square miles of the United States will be seen daily in many metropolitan areas.

The cities we encounter will continue to become more complex, structured, and difficult to manage. To experience cities will be to experience sensory overload. Richard Wurman in his book, *Information Anxiety,* helps us to understand this. As a designer of guidebooks for cities he indicates that "cities don't come in chapters with restaurants in one section and museums in another; their order is organic, sometimes confusing, never alphabetic. To really experience a city fully, you have to acknowledge confusion."[1] We will have increasing difficulty understanding cities in order to plan missions strategies targeting the lost, unchurched, and hurting people.

Christian denominations and groups continue to search for the most effective urban church strategies. As will be seen from the twelve challenges, this is a moving target, and will mean different things for different denominations and groups throughout the next generation.

The Challenge of Strategic Vision

The challenge upon which all other challenges rest is strategic vision. Many Christians are committed to sharing the good news with residents of cities. However, they may not have a vision of a process for effectively sharing the gospel in ways which will make kingdom progress over a sustained period of time.

A strategic vision involves two things. First, it is the ability to articulate the dream, purpose, or mission of the individual or group. A vision means that a clear, concise sense of direction is well known by all who are involved in the leadership of the movement. The question of why church-growth activities are being engaged in does not come up. Everyone knows the validity of actions because of the common commitment to kingdom progress.

Second, the willingness to focus on activities which will yield the greatest progress over a period of time, according to an agreed-upon plan or framework, is strategic commitment. Short-term gains and projects favored by some individuals are set aside in favor of planning processes and programs which yield greater long-term results.

For example, mass evangelism projects may be discussed, but only implemented if they can yield the same results as, or better results than, incremental personal evangelism efforts. Strategic thinking will take into account whether the resources available in a particular setting favor new congregational development or strengthening the outreach of existing congregations.

Individuals, congregations, missions groups, and denominations must begin their journey of effective urban mission strategy by spending sufficient time to develop and articulate a strategic vision, or sense of mission, directed toward the cities. Without such a vision much time and resources may be wasted by persons and groups who, although busy in Christian ministry, lack a focus to their activities.

Many persons and groups possess the raw materials needed to address effectively the spiritual hunger of the cities. However, they have no sense of how to use these resources in an organized way to accomplish the Great Commission. This crucial difference cannot always be measured. It must be felt as spiritual intuition.

The Challenge of Demographics

Society is so inundated by numbers that at times they become meaningless. This is true particularly when the numbers are too large to comprehend. Such may be the case when consideration is given to the largest metropolitan areas of the world. The challenge of demographics is to interpret their meaning for us, and to suggest actions we ought to take in light of their meaning.

Missions researcher David Barrett has assisted the Foreign Mission Board of the Southern Baptist Convention in giving meaning to many of the large numbers associated with understanding the world's largest metropolitan areas. Placing cities in categories is one way to deal with the confusion and frustration of comprehending massive numbers of people whom we cannot know personally, but care about as a result our own spiritual regeneration.

Barrett suggests that we ought to begin any serious discussion of cities with those which have a population of at least one million. Cities of this size are known as megacities. Beyond this level, cities of over four million are supercities, and those over ten million in population are supergiants.[2] These supergiants will range in size from approximately 18 million to 34 million.[3]

A major challenge of demographics relates to the increase in urban dwellers worldwide, as compared to the penetration of the gospel among the world's population. Research shows that in 1990 urban dwellers accounted for 45 percent of the world's population. By the end of the next generation, urban dwellers will have increased their share of the world population to 60 percent.[4]

In 1990 Christianity accounted for 45 percent of the world's population. If current trends continue, only 43 percent of the world's population will embrace Christianity in the year 2015.[5]

An "adequate" strategic vision is not sufficient when confronted by the realities of demographics. Only remarkable effort will reverse current trends, because even though the number of Christians will increase substantially during the next generation, the percentage of the population which is Christian will decline.

In the United States, besides the two supergiants of New York City and Los Angeles, the urban challenge includes eight supercities and thirty-four megacities. The eight supercities are Chicago, San Francisco, Philadelphia, Houston, Boston, Detroit, Dallas-Fort Worth, and Washington, D.C. One challenge of demographics is to discover how we can concentrate resources and attention on the areas where a large percentage of the people live.

The Challenge of National and Global Strategies

National and international missions organizations have a responsibility to develop a framework in which local and regional strategies can be developed. The challenge is to establish a framework focused enough to provide guidance for the development and distribution of necessary resources yet flexible enough to allow for strategies adapted to local situations.

Larry McSwain of The Southern Baptist Theological Seminary in Louisville, Kentucky, indicates that "what a denomination can do is to focus its energies upon its historical giftedness to make those contributions to the wholeness of the city's people most consistent with its resources and traditions."[6]

In terms of national missions, what Southern Baptists have done is to establish a strategy framework called Mega Focus Cities to focus attention upon the megacities, supercities, and supergiants.

This author was part of the team which put Mega Focus Cities together for the Home Mission Board of the Southern Baptist Convention during 1981. It was conceived, not as a national strategy, but as a national strategy framework from which customized strategies, highly relevant to their metropolitan setting, could be developed by local associations of churches.

The role of the national agency is to act as catalyst for the research and planning process, and then to assist with networks and linkages to provide the resources to implement the locally owned, custom-made, and open-ended strategies.

The principles of a strategy framework function equally well for international missions organizations. Observation of the strategic suggestions by such organizations indicates that they are looking at some of the same type of processes. David Barrett, who has observed many international strategies, indicates that "to be successful, any strategy of global evangelization must set goals that are possible, feasible, reachable, accessible, and capable of being implemented."[7]

The implied challenge for national and global strategies is that they will not necessarily involve the unusual and the dramatic, but will focus upon innovative and creative use of the resources at hand. Effective and efficient implementation and execution of good plans is more important than excellent plans which cannot be implemented with a reasonable resource base.

The Challenge of Leadership

Longevity of ministry, a key issue in metropolitan church leadership, necessitates a high degree of comfort in working in the city with the people of the city. The cities of the world need persons called to Christian ministry who feel comfortable with the city, and who see it as a place where they can put down roots. The peace of the city and their personal peace need to be intertwined. As in all ministry, there will be days when only a sense of spiritual call sustain a minister amid the pressures and emotions of the city.

The challenge of leadership is to discover processes to train, place, orient, and support excellent leaders to serve in critical places of metropolitan leadership. This cannot be done informally. A system must be established which discovers ministers early in their training who can be prepared for unique service in the cities.

Missions structures have failed to provide empowerment to ministers who have been sent to the cities to serve. As a result, short tenure, ineffective service, or burnout has been experienced by these ministers. Ministers cannot lead in their settings, with a strategic vision, in response to a national strategy framework unless they are sufficiently trained, appropriately placed, fully oriented, and then properly supported by peers, local networks, and denominational linkages.

Twenty-five years ago G. Willis Bennett of The Southern Baptist Theological Seminary conducted benchmark research on ministry in the city for the Home Mission Board, SBC. He saw a few pastors cry when telling about failure and frustration in the midst of the city.[8]

Further, about 80 percent of the more than one hundred pastors of churches in metropolitan transition whom Bennett interviewed recognized that their churches would not be able to reach the variety of people in the community around them unless they could expand or change the church programs and activities.[9] Twenty-five years ago Southern Baptists did not offer many resources to assist these pastors in making these changes. Now they do. This is a part of the empowerment of leadership which must continue.

Another element of the challenge of leadership relates to laypersons. The training and motivation of volunteers is essential to the successful accomplishment of effective urban church strategies. Full-time ministers cannot be provided for all the places which need ministry assistance. Laypersons are a major resource of leadership. Models of ministry must be developed which utilize them. Too many ministry models assume a full-time professional minister will be present to implement it. In increasing numbers of places, this will not be true.

Leadership development programs which target the full-time professional minister and laypersons who can function as ministers, need to be established close to major metropolitan areas. Existing seminaries and divinity schools can modify their curriculum and degree offerings to accommodate this need. Models for ministry education which are mobile and specialized are emerging, and should be encouraged.

The Challenge of Congregations

Since the first-century church was established, Christianity has expanded by developing new congregations. This approach is proper.

One challenge of congregations is to keep the focus upon local congregations where people can worship God together and grow spiritually in the midst of a caring, loving fellowship. The primary Christian relationship found in a local congregation has no substitute.

A more difficult challenge of congregations is working in a balanced way with every congregation to affirm its kingdom strength. Most churches can be placed in one of three categories: newly developing congregations, established congregations which are growing, or established congregations which are plateaued or declining.

Each category of congregations has unique needs which must be met by the larger fellowship of Christianity. Strategically, however, one category cannot dominate another. Methods must be found to assist each type of church in moving forward in the areas of its strengths.

Growing congregations need affirmation to keep growing. The best way they can grow in quantity and quality may be to start a new congregation in an area of need and provide core members for the new congregation from their own membership.

Plateaued and declining congregations need affirmation that their situation may have external as well as internal causes, and their vision of renewed ministry is possible. The challenge is to help these congregations understand that cosmetic changes in building and programs will probably not be sufficient. Bold directions will be needed in many cases to grasp a new sense of spiritual and strategic direction. Only a minority of these congregations will hear this challenge. If a plateaued or declining congregation "must perpetuate the status quo, doing the same things in the same ways for the same people, the church may find its life threatened and its ministry most ineffective."[10]

New congregational development needs to remain the top priority in an effective urban church strategy. It may not always be popular, but it must always be accomplished prophetically and with risk taking. "On the basis of urban population growth alone, therefore, churches are challenged to make an unprecedented expansion of facilities, services, and number of new churches. Any major denomination needs a careful plan for church extension."[11]

The Challenge of Growth

Being busy about missions activity does not necessarily produce long-term missions growth. This is true whether the activity is ministry, evangelism, new congregational development, or the growth of existing churches. This is particularly true if any of these activities are implemented in isolation from one another.

What is needed is a holistic approach to congregational-based metropolitan strategy. (See fig. A.) This approach suggests that ministry, evangelism, new congregational development, and the growth of existing churches are different phases of an overall church-growth strategy. Each plays an important role in a growth process.

These phases form a cycle which can repeat itself as each succeeding strategy is completed. Also, each cycle can begin with any of the four strategy elements. The entry point for strategy implementation in a certain city or neighborhood may be at the point of ministry, evangelism, new congregational development, or the growth of existing congregations. Each situation will be different.

For example, several years ago an evangelism strategist suggested to a church group in Philadelphia a direct evangelism approach in an inner-city neighborhood. The group in Philadelphia knew that the

FIGURE A

A HOLISTIC CYCLE OF CHURCH-BASED
METROPOLITAN STRATEGY

Entry
Point

EVANGELISM →

NEW CONGREGATIONS

Entry
Point

MINISTRY

CHURCH-BASED
METROPOLITAN
STRATEGY

Entry
Point

GROWTH OF
EXISTING CHURCHES

Entry
Point

better approach was to enter the community at the point of cultivating ministry, and then move expeditiously to the direct evangelism approach as the second phase of the strategy.

Larry McSwain emphasized the need for a holistic growth strategy in Houston and other Sunbelt cities when he implied that evangelism and new congregational development should lead to growing congregations who out of their maturity reach out to the community around them. He emphasized this by suggesting that "the failure to choose a growth priority as one's strategy for the future is tantamount to choosing for an increasingly secular, unchurched or sectarian moral environment."[12]

The crucial challenge is for churches and missions organizations to be involved in all types of growth activities with lost, unchurched, and hurting people. "The churches in the city which are accomplishing the most and are making the greatest appeal to people today are the churches which are more totally involved in the lives of people."[13]

The holistic approach to congregational-based metropolitan strategy blurs the lines between ministry, evangelism, new congregational development, and the growth of existing churches. It allows churches and missions organizations to take an integrative approach in the city. It asserts that "a program of Christian ministry that demonstrates a congregation's willingness to give themselves in service to a community is clearly evangelistic."[14]

The Challenge of Race and Ethnicity

Race and ethnicity present a formidable challenge to the movement of Christianity throughout the world. The past thirty years have brought significant progress toward ethnic and racial diversity among Christian groups in America.

Individual congregations have successfully addressed issues of integration during the past generation. The next generation has almost unlimited potential for growth of the Christian church in America among non-Anglo groups.

However, the challenge to the traditional, Anglo church is great.

Asians, Hispanics, and Afro-Americans outnumber Anglos in twenty-five American cities of 100,000 or more in population.

One of every three Afro-Americans in the United States lives in one of six cities: New York, Los Angeles, Chicago, Philadelphia, Detroit, or Washington, D. C. One of every two persons of Hispanic origin lives in one of five cities: Los Angeles, New York, San Francisco, Chicago, or Miami.[15] The challenge is to see these numbers, where the people are located, and to develop strategies to reach those who are lost, unchurched, and hurting with the good news.

For Southern Baptists the greatest challenge during the next generation will be among Afro-Americans. In recent years this denomination has radically changed its strategy among Afro-Americans from one which focuses upon relationships with black Baptist groups, to a proactive strategy of starting new congregations in predominately black communities. Already there are about 1,300 predominately black Southern Baptist congregations. Within the next generation there could easily be over 5,000 such congregations.

This is only one example of the diversification in what is now the most ethnically diverse non-Catholic group in the United States. Southern Baptists worship and minister each week in about ninety different language culture groupings.

The Challenge of Life-style

America is not as simple a place as it used to be. American people live much more diverse life-styles than ever before. Marketing research now identifies and targets several dozens distinguishable life-styles throughout the nation.

The Christian church has generally not kept pace with the ability to identify the various life-styles which exist in America. The challenge of life-style is to use available research to assist in developing strategies to reach target groups which may otherwise remain hidden to the casual Christian witness. These identifiable life-style groups are determined by multiple variables such as age, income, education, occupation, household size, and location and type of residence.

Looking at age as one variable, we discover America is aging so rapidly that this challenge will significantly affect church life immediately and for the next two generations. In July 1983 the number of Americans over the age of fifty-six surpassed the number of teenagers.[16] The cities of America will be the location of many of the more than forty million Americans who will be over the age of sixty-five by the year 2000.

The Challenge of Resources

Resources to do missions work in the cities of America and the world are not a problem. They are available. The problem is that too many people see money as the only resource. The challenge of resources is to expand the concept of what is a resource, and how it is gathered, developed, and distributed.

Among the resources which should be considered are money, people, buildings, materials, equipment, research, and creativity. Money, people, buildings, materials, and equipment are common resources which are generally considered when putting together a comprehensive list of resources.

Research is a challenging resource. It relates to the fact that many times churches and missions organizations engage in strategies which have not been thoroughly investigated, tested, and are not regularly evaluated. Available resources are wasted on ineffective strategies.

Research will increase the resources which can be focused upon crucial, difficult target groups in the cities. The size and complexity of cities can cause large amounts of resources to be disbursed. If inadequate research causes resources to be wasted, then the challenge of effectively utilizing resources has not been successfully met.

Creativity is an important part of the resource picture. Frequently missions administrators know only one right way to distribute available resources. Creativity assists in discovering numerous ways to accomplish the same objective. So important is creativity to the process of conserving resources, that no strategy should be implemented unless at least two others ways of accomplishing the same strategy can be put forth by those making the strategic proposal.

Through creativity new ways will be found to penetrate the cities of America and the world with the gospel. Without a bias toward creativity, old strategies which have outlived their usefulness and effectiveness will continue to be implemented. Even among the common resources, such as buildings, much misunderstanding exists as to their necessity and proper use. In many cities a church is not considered fully developed unless it has a building of its own. This attitude is challenged in a city like Boston where the cost of land and buildings is out of reach for many congregations.

By 1995 there will be about seventy-five Southern Baptist congregations in the greater Boston area. It is likely that no more than twenty of these congregations will have their own building. Creative approaches to providing space for congregational activities allow these congregations to be growing, maturing bodies of believers without a building of their own.

The Challenge of Networks and Linkages

The task of sharing the good news with the cities of America and the world is enormous. Therefore, it cannot be accomplished alone. Local, regional, national, and global missions agencies need to respond to the challenge of networking with other similar organizations, and linking with other missions groups within their own denomination.

At the local level, "cooperation must exist between congregations in the city so as to strengthen the work of a specific congregation located in a particular area."[17] This cooperation can involve establishing networks of information within a city among congregations and missions groups involved in similar strategy areas. Cooperation can also involve establishing linkages between suburban congregations and central city congregations.

Networks and linkages should be developed either within the same denominational group, or if they are across denominational lines they should be considered interdenominational as opposed to ecumenical.

The difference between the two is more than semantics.

Ecumenical relationships can involve the loss of denominational identity and can potentially weaken strategic efforts as tactics move to the least common denominator between the participating denominations. These relationships may be called linkages because of the development of interdependent relationships.

Interdenominational networks involve exchanging information concerning plans and programs, and some agreements which call for one denomination to focus, for example, on hunger, and another on refugees. However, there is no loss of the strengths of any denominational group because each is free to pursue its own strategic vision.

The Challenge of Local Strategies

At the local level, the challenge is to take the combined influence of all the previous challenges, and put in place detailed strategies for making kingdom progress in the setting where God has called the church, association, or local judicatory. A comprehensive, cohesive, and correlated strategy planning process is needed by each church or missions group.

"Strategy planning involves identifying those decisions which can be made which potentially can effect the achieving of established goals and directions within an organization. The primary objective of this process is to collect in a comprehensive way the necessary information by which specific decisions can be identified by a planning group which will allow the planning group to work more effectively in the future . . . ." in its setting.[18]

In regard to the Southern Baptist strategy mentioned earlier called Mega Focus Cities, forty-four cities throughout the United States will, during the decade of the 1990s, be presented with the framework which the national and regional structures have provided them. From this they will develop the locally owned, custom-made, and open-ended strategies to respond to missions needs in their metropolitan setting.

The major areas which these strategies will address are predictable.

They will likely include a focus upon evangelism, ministry, new congregational development, strengthening existing congregations, leadership training, communication, fellowship, and organizational development.

A high degree of ownership of the direction and details of these strategies by the local congregations is essential. In fact, a strong sense of ownership is the primary challenge of developing local strategies. The congregations will be responsible for implementation. They must feel that the agreed-upon strategies represent God's will for their congregation in the city, or the strategies become no more than documents for historical reference.

The Challenge of Theology

By far the greatest challenge involved in reaching the cities is a theological one. "Lost people in the cities have sent a Macedonian call to come and witness, to develop mission-minded churches and to minister in Christ's name."[19] The Christian church must be mobilized by a theology which actively embraces all the lost, unchurched, and hurting people of the cities.

In the United States almost ninety million lost people live in the forty-four Mega Focus Cities. This means that over 70 percent of the population of these cities are lost.[20] In light of the Great Commission, Christians heed the truth of these figures. "As long as masses of people remain outside the church, congregations ought to have a concern about evangelism and growth."[21]

The theology of the church must be inclusive in order to be effective in the city. "Paul's strategy was based upon the assumption that every person in a geographic region ought to have the opportunity to experience the gospel. Thus, he developed an organizational pattern which would potentially meet such a goal."[22]

Conclusion

Throughout the next generation, the success of Christianity will depend upon how well the missions needs of the cities of the world are met. From now through the year 2015 if Christian denominations and groups respond positively to the twelve challenges, then they will have discovered effective urban strategy and implementation.

The hope found only in Jesus Christ can best be shared by the church on mission in the cities of the world. The Christian church must serve as a compelling source of hope for our cities.

Notes

1. Richard Saul Wurman, *Information Anxiety* (New York: Doubleday, 1989), 48.

2. David B. Barrett, *World-Class Cities and World Evangelization* (Birmingham, Alabama: New Hope, 1986), 8.

3. Barrett, 49.

4. Ibid., 16.

5. Ibid.

6. Larry L. McSwain, "Touching Houston for Christ: Mission Strategy in The Sunbelt City," June 8, 1984 (unpublished paper), 10.

7. Barrett, 30.

8. G. Willis Bennett, *Confronting a Crisis* (Atlanta: Home Mission Board, 1967), 22.

9. Ibid., 26.

10. Ibid., 41.

11. Ibid., 86.

12. McSwain, 74.

13. Bennett, *Confronting a Crisis,* 83.

14. G. Willis Bennett, *Effective Urban Church Ministry* (Nashville: Broadman Press, 1983), 114.

15. Research Division, "The Largest United States Metropolitan Areas by the Year 2000," (Atlanta: Home Mission Board, SBC, March 10, 1987), 3.

16. Ken Dychtwald and Joe Flower, *Age Wave* (Los Angeles: Jeremy P. Tarcher, 1989), 8.

17. Bennett, *Confronting a Crisis,* 81.

18. McSwain, 11.

19. W. Jere Allen, "Metro Focus," in Associational Missions Division, *Associational Bulletin,* vol. 23, no. 2, March/April 1989 (Atlanta: Home Mission Board, SBC, 1989), 7.

20. Research Division, 8.

21. Bennett, *Effective Urban Church Ministry,* 107.

22. McSwain, 7.

||| 6 |||

Long-Range Planning in the Local Church
by Michael J. Clingenpeel

Social change is an axiom of contemporary American life. The pace of change is increasing rapidly. Much change is unplanned, and some argue it is unwanted. Virtually every community and institution is affected in subtle or significant ways by social flux.

Churches are no exception. Congregations are local expressions of the body of Christ. They are also social systems with complex networks of relationships and structures, formal and informal. Congregations are living organisms, dynamic and everchanging. "Will my church change?" is not a realistic question. The accurate question is "Will my congregation's change be planned or unplanned?"

Churches occasionally react to fast change with frantic activity. Wrote one wag:

> Mary had a little lamb,
> It would have been a sheep,
> But it went and joined a Baptist church
> And died from lack of sleep.

Activity without direction is not only frantic, it is fruitless. It is ministry by accident rather than design.

The premise of this chapter is that long-range planning is an essential task of a healthy congregation in our swiftly shifting society. In the following pages long-range planning will be defined and its process described. The role of the pastor in and the benefits of long-range planning also will be considered.

Long-Range Planning Defined

Long-range planning is the process by which a congregation analyzes itself and its setting in order to understand its larger mission, define its specific identity, and develop tangible strategies to fulfill its goals.

What is meant by "long-range" varies, with community being the key variable that determines the optimum time frame for a long-range plan. Churches located in communities undergoing rapid change, particularly high population transition, may not be able to plan beyond three to five years. Even this may require less specific strategies and annual review and alteration of the plan. Churches in stable localities may be able to set realistic strategies up to ten years. Projections beyond ten years are more appropriately called "dreams" than "plans," though it is certainly excellent to have them. Generally the longer the plan projects into the future, the more general the plan and the strategies to achieve it must be.

Long-range planning is to a church what a thermostat is to a home.[1] A thermostat controls the environment, a thermometer records it. Healthy congregations need an instrument that will stabilize the environment despite the roller-coaster extremes occurring outside it. Unhealthy congregations allow environmental changes occurring around them to control what they do. Healthy congregations make things happen. Unhealthy congregations react to what happens.

Long-range planning in churches presents a fascinating paradox. It is easiest and most accurate where the environment is stable and predictability is high. Yet it is more necessary for organizational effectiveness where the environment is complex and volatile.[2]

The Process of Long-Range Planning

The stages in the long-range planning process are not rigidly defined. No one recipe for planning is gospel.[3] Nonetheless, two basic ingredients are common to virtually all long-range planning processes: definition of congregational mission and identity and development of tangible strategies for meeting agreed-upon goals.

Definition of Congregational Mission and Identity

Every local church which attempts to define its larger mission and specific identity must begin by asking a series of simple, yet probing questions:

1. Who are we?
2. Where are we?
3. What are we doing?
4. What should we be doing?

When these questions are honestly and objectively answered, a congregation will have a clearer picture of its mission and identity.

1. In an effort to answer the question "who are we?" the long-range planning process begins with a reexamination of the mission of the church. Emil Brunner wrote: "The church exists by mission just as a fire exists by burning. Where there is no mission there is no Church."[4] Without mission a church has no direction, objective, or foundation. Initiating the planning process with a review and reaffirmation of mission provides the biblical/theological foundation for a congregation's existence and plans for the future.

The basic mission of the church is to glorify God by making Him known through Jesus Christ. This mission is always and everywhere the same. To fulfill this mission churches must fulfill at least five functions: proclamation/evangelism, worship, education/nurture, fellowship, and service/ministry. In one way or another every local church should fulfill these functions.

Some statement of a church's reason for being should be included in the development of its long-range plan. This statement reflects an understanding of the mission of the church and becomes the standard by which all specific ministries are measured. When any one of the above five functions is not addressed with a specific strategy for ministry, a strategy should be formulated to address this aspect of mission. When any specific form of ministry, by congregational consensus, cannot be considered to fulfill one of these functions, that ministry should be eliminated. In this way a local church does not stray far from its God-given mission.

2. Once a statement of mission is clearly articulated, the planning process must answer the question "where are we?" The answer to this question is found by researching and describing the communities with which the church is identified. Local churches are part of geographic, relational, and denominational communities. Understanding these social, congregational, and denominational contexts is an essential stage in the formulation of congregational identity.

The destiny of any church is inextricably linked to its geographic setting. Its immediate community sets limits upon and creates opportunities for a church's ministry. To overlook one's geographic setting will leave a church ignorant of the primary target area for its ministry. Some attempt must be made to analyze the institutions, social processes, demographics, and ethos of the area immediately surrounding the church. A long-range planning committee will find many sources for such information, including planning data from local governments and agencies, census data, personal observation, and business forecasts.

A second community of utmost importance is the church membership itself. The character of the church membership must be scrutinized carefully along the lines of age, gender, tenure of membership, and participation patterns. Perceptions of members about their church's programs and overall effectiveness also can be instructive in understanding and shaping identity. Methods can be found to form congregational identity by eliciting the dreams and aspirations of church members.

Care should be taken when performing this type of congregational research. Church surveys should be designed to avoid requesting information that is unnecessary and unusable in formulating the long-range plan. Short questionnaires are more likely to receive a good response and prevent the planning committee from being overwhelmed with interesting, but obscure, data. Canned research instruments may appear thorough and easy to use but are not likely to fit the needs of every congregation. One size does not fit all. When these pitfalls are avoided, congregational research is an innovative way for understanding the relational community.[5]

Most churches are affiliated with a denominational family which shapes or reflects their identity. Longstanding denominational commitments are important facts of a church's identity and must be considered in any long-term plan. The strength of a church's denominational identity and commitment has significant implications for its budget and program ministries.

This matrix of geographic, relational, and denominational factors helps define the identity of a local church. A church which knows "where" it is better understands "who" it is and "what" it ought to be doing.

3. Having articulated its mission and defined its community, a local church must answer the question "what are we doing?" Any church maintains a variety of programs and specific ministries that demand the time and financial support of its members. No process of planning is complete until the effectiveness of all programs is analyzed. A planning process must look carefully at each ministry it performs so that at a fixed point in time a congregation can estimate the scope and nature of its witness.

One method for program evaluation is to list every program of the church under categories corresponding with the five functions of the church listed earlier in this chapter. Most programs will fit clearly under one of these functions. This list will be helpful when matching present program with needs and resources.

Some programs are integral to the identity of a congregation. A church located adjacent to a major college or university, and whose membership consists largely of students and university employees, cannot eliminate programs attractive to students without significantly altering the identity of the church. Adding, restructuring, or eliminating programs is a realistic result of any long-range planning process, but every church should be alert to the way in which such changes will shape its identity.

4. After addressing the issues of mission, community, and program, those doing long-range planning must ask the question "What should we be doing?" This will require a committee to analyze apparent needs and available resources to meet those needs. The specific ministry strategies of any church are in large measure defined by documented, unmet needs and available resources. When sufficient study of a church's community is complete, almost always unmet human needs are revealed. Needs constitute opportunities for ministry.

Here a congregation must be careful. Needs may be present that are being addressed by several other churches or community organizations. It is unnecessary to compete with other groups to meet a need that is being addressed adequately while other clear needs go unaddressed.

Needs also may be uncovered which a local church does not have the human or financial resources to meet effectively. This may call a church to unite its resources with other churches or community groups to meet a need.

It may also represent an area of need a congregation must bypass. One local church cannot be all things to all people, nor do all things for all people. Each church must define its specific strengths and special calling. No church should feel that it must duplicate the services of every other church. Not every church is a supermarket, stocking every imaginable item. Many are specialty shops which provide a limited, but excellent, range of ministries.[6]

The answer to the question "what should we be doing?" requires the careful blending of needs assessment with resource development. Where needs are pressing and resources can be acquired, a strategy for ministry must be developed.

Development of Tangible Strategies for Ministry

Once a congregation has completed its self-assessment and has a clear sense of its mission and identity, it must move to develop definite strategies for the fulfillment of its mission. A long-range plan does not exist until specific strategies are offered which address needs within and outside a church. This second major stage in the long-range planning process answers the question "what is the best way to do what we should be doing?" The following principles should be considered in strategy development:

1. Strategies for ministry should be specific. A planning committee, for example, may reach the conclusion that "our members do not believe we are evangelistic as we should be." But this assessment takes no tangible step toward strengthening the evangelistic ministry of the congregation. A more specific strategy would be to recommend that "once each year for the next five years our evangelism committee will plan a seminar to train church members in personal witnessing."

Such specific strategies have the advantage of being easily understood by church staff and committees. They also can be evaluated unequivocally. They enable a church to know that it is taking measurable strides toward the fulfillment of its mission and is addressing a perceived need of its members.

Any specific strategy should include a church staff member, committee, or structure assigned with responsibility for its implementation. Whether the strategy is implemented through established organizations of the local church or through some special structure is a matter of congregational preference, but a stated channel for implementation is essential.

The same principle applies to the method for periodic evaluation of the complete long-range plan. A process for review of the plan should be included in the final plan. This allows for flexibility and adjustment of ministry strategies to accommodate changing needs and opportunities for ministry.

2. At its best, long-range planning is holistic. Therefore, strategies should be developed for all facets of a church's ministry, including programming, finances and budgeting, physical property and facilities, staff, and denominational relationships. Enlarging the scope of planning to include all aspects of congregational life enables a fuller coordination of priorities and ministries.

3. Strategies must be creative, fresh, challenging. Where careful assessment reveals current programs and strategies meeting documented needs, they should be continued and affirmed. But old needs often require new methods to address them. Though the basic mission of the church doesn't change, the strategies for fulfilling this mission vary with time and the changing context of ministry. New wineskins must be put in place to carry the old wine of the gospel. Congregations must not be afraid to develop fresh and even risky strategies as a part of their goals to reach a briskly changing environment.

4. Strategies should have congregational ownership. In churches with congregational polity it is essential that the planning process include a method for making church members "stakeholders" in the action plans.[7] People who have little input into the final long-term plan for their church are unlikely to feel ownership of the plan, and therefore are less likely to feel wedded to its recommendations.

This can be achieved without making the church business meeting a "committee-of-the-whole," an action that can become unwieldy or chaotic. Maximum input in the planning process can occur through a variety of methods, including interviews with individual church members, listening sessions with small groups of church members, and congregational surveys of the leadership corps or sample of the total membership. Presentation of the long-range plan in a business meeting, allowing for amendments and adoption of the plan, can generate enthusiasm and foster a healthy sense of ownership which pays dividends as the plan is implemented. How a local church arrives at a sense of ownership of its long-range plan is a matter where each seeks its own comfort, but in most Baptist congregations a plan should be "from below up" rather than "from above down."

5. The formulation of strategies can be enhanced by the services of an outside consultant. A trained consultant may bring a broader perspective to the process which increases the awareness of the range of ministry strategies available to a church. A consultant often is able to interpret the information collected during the planning process with greater objectivity than church staff or laypersons. Obviously mem-

bers may accept or reject the consultant's interpretation and recommendations. But inviting no assistance almost ensures a more limited assessment of the facts and possibilities. In any long-range planning process a congregation may need to hear assessments of its ministry that cannot be offered by a pastor or fellow members with the candor that a respected consultant can offer. Seminaries and denominational offices are good sources for recommendations when a church wants to find a consultant.

When a church has defined its mission and prepared its strategies to fulfill its mission, the long-range plan is ready for implementation. Note that this process of planning goes from ends to means rather than means to ends, from general to specific rather than specific to general, from biblical/theological to practical rather than practical to biblical/theological. Only after sound biblical/theological foundation of the mission of the church and clear definition of congregational identity are set forth are specific strategies for ministry proposed.

Both stages in the process are essential. An understanding of the mission of the church without strategies for its accomplishment is like having blueprints without building materials and a contractor to do the work. A series of mission strategies without a biblical/theological basis is like lumber, bricks, and contractor without a blueprint. But when both are present, that which is in the mind of the Designer can become reality.

The Role of the Pastor in Long-Range Planning

The pastor of a local church plays a key role in the initiation, development, and implementation of a long-range plan. In theory it is possible for a congregation to develop a long-range plan without the support of a pastor. But in practice this is rarely the case.

The role of a pastor in long-range planning is essentially that of "helper." The pastor gently nudges the congregation in the direction of its dreams and purposes. Before the process of long-range planning has congregational acceptance, a pastor can point out the values of planning. The pastor may initiate a proposal to the church's governing board or council that the congregation enter a period of self-study and goal setting. Individual conversations with church members are fertile opportunities to affirm the value of planning for the church's future.

Once the planning process has begun formally a pastor may take an active role in assisting a long-range planning committee with its work. Within the planning committee and in corporate worship a pastor can articulate the biblical/theological foundation for the mission of the church, and challenge the congregation with its mandate to address human needs in its community. A pastor may share perceptions of needs and suggest strategies gleaned from personal experience and the experiences of other churches addressing similar needs in similar settings.

After the plan is approved for implementation a pastor must keep the plan before the congregation, channeling its recommendations to proper committees for implementation and evaluation, and scheduling periodic celebrations when portions of the plan are completed.

Pastors must guard against forcing their own personal vision for the church upon the members. God may provide a dream to a pastor, but the pastor cannot remain the sole repository of the plan. It must become a shared dream of the congregation. In the process a pastor must be open to seeing the dream take a different shape under the analysis of the planning process and the application of congregational insights.

This implies that long-range planning is a process that works best where "consensus leadership" is the pastoral style. Authoritarian leadership leaves little room for shared vision and congregational input. While it does not preclude planning by definition, it devalues the principle of ownership of congregational goals.

The Benefits of Long-Range Planning

At the beginning of this chapter it was stated that long-range planning is an essential task of a healthy congregation in our swiftly changing society. Not everyone would agree.[8] It has been argued that long-range planning robs a congregation of its creativity, spontaneity, and stifles the movement of the Holy Spirit. Some suggest that planning sets limits upon God by narrowing a congregation's focus to local needs and ready resources. Some critics of long-range planning view triage, choosing to focus on some needs while turning away from others, as an unnecessary and unhealthy limitation of God's power. Planning is rejected by others as being overly concerned with survival and structures and too little focused upon mission and ministries.

Any of these scenarios can occur in churches where the process of long-range planning becomes an end in itself rather than a means to more effective and broader ministry. But they need not happen. The potential benefits of long-range planning far surpass the assumed risks.

A long-range plan provides an action plan for a congregation and its staff. When a congregation has adopted a long-range plan that is holistic and has measurable strategies, a pastor and staff have specific direction for their daily work which they sense has the support of the people who have issued their call to that local church. While pastoral ministry from a servant perspective by its very nature must be reactive occasionally, pastoral ministry with a long-range plan is predominantly proactive. One can plan work according to agreed-upon goals and strategies, reducing the loss of purpose or significance that haunts pastoral ministry.

This action plan is especially helpful in the repetitive and often mundane administrative tasks of a congregation. The plan provides a larger framework for decision making in annual budgeting, programming, organizational structure, facilities management, and personnel supervision and employment. It leaves far less to chance, risk, and whim. With social change occurring at a gallop, every significant congregational decision involves some risk. A long-range plan does not eliminate risk, but by anticipating problems the plan increases the probability that proper decisions are made.

Used appropriately by church staff and laity, a long-range plan is an excellent tool of outreach. Many prospective church members want to know a church's identity and direction before joining. Buttressed by a thorough long-range plan, a pastor can confidently say to a prospect: "This is who our congregation perceives itself to be, and this is what we are committed to do." Prospective members can then choose the church based upon their desire to enter into the life of a congregation with its specific strengths, weaknesses, and commitments. It also will enable some prospects to eliminate the church from their consideration because it does not offer the kind of programs and church life they find meaningful, a fact which spares hurt feelings over unfulfilled expectations.

A long-range plan sharpens a congregation's self-awareness and self-esteem, both of which are as important to churches as to individuals. By preventing a congregation from constantly reacting to environmental pressures and changes, a long-range plan removes the oppressive sense of being out of control, helpless against the currents and eddies of social change. Each time a specific strategy is implemented successfully, church members and staff experience the satisfaction of a task accomplished. Celebration of these small victories strengthens the faith needed to accept greater challenges as a congregation and staff. As a by-product, the heightening of congregational self-esteem forges a stronger bond between pastor and people, which increases the likelihood of more effective corporate ministry.

Long-range planning is not the thief of serendipity in congregational life. Planning need not steal from a church the spontaneity of the Holy Spirit. When a congregation sees itself as a living body of believers empowered by a dynamic God who is continually being revealed in new and vital ways in the lives of people and communities, planning can become the vehicle through which the Holy Spirit speaks and leads a community of believers. Serendipity is achieved through planning.

Notes

1. This analogy is used by Kenneth J. Kilinski and Jerry C. Wofford, *Organization and Leadership in the Local Church* (Grand Rapids: Zondervan Publishing House,

1973), 186-87.

2. The paradox of planning is discussed in Jeff Clark, "Planning: The Cure for Organizational Motion Sickness," *Search* 11 (Winter 1981): 6.

3. To sample stages in long-range planning recommended by others see Kilinski and Wofford, 186-91; G. Willis Bennett, *Guidelines for Effective Urban Church Ministry* (Nashville: Broadman Press, 1983), 17-24; Robert T. Dale, *To Dream Again* (Nashville: Broadman Press, 1981), 63-75, 129-47; Clark, 6-13; Don J. McMinn, "Strategic Planning in the Local Church: Option or Imperative," *Search* 15 (Winter 1985): 28-37.

4. Emil Brunner, *The Word and the World* (London: SCM Press, 1931), 108.

5. For a thorough and practical discussion of congregational research see James F. Engel, "Sidestepping Pitfalls in Congregational Research," *Leadership* 5 (Winter 1984): 26-29.

6. This analogy was used by Marshall Shelley, "What's a Body to Do?" *Leadership* 5 (Winter 1984): 43.

7. The term "stakeholders" is used effectively by Dale, 66.

8. To sample some objections see Clark, 14 and Shelley, 43.

||| 7 |||

Serving the Transitional Community Church
by Edward B. Freeman, Jr.

In Southern Baptist life and in the larger circles of American Christianity, there is no greater challenge or more ominous threat than ministry in transitional community churches. All over America, especially in older residential neighborhoods and in the core areas of our cities, churches are dying, victims of inability to cope with the sociological and demographic changes of the transitional communities around them.

All communities are transitional. No community remains static. For purposes of this essay, however, the terms "transitional community" and "transitional community church" focus on those situations in which the interaction between church and community leads to institutional decline.

Population shifts have affected whole communities and churches. Rural churches decline and die because their people have moved to the city. Rural churches on the urban fringe lapse into conflict over attempts to adapt their ministries to the life-style of the new suburbanites in their backyards. Older neighborhood churches, minus their younger adults who have moved out, struggle to maintain their ministries with a constituency now both smaller and older. Churches in the city core awake to the reality of no community at all as commercial development replaces formerly residential neighborhoods. Common to all these types of churches is a severe difficulty in dealing with neighborhood change.

These factors make serving the transitional community church one of the most difficult assignments in the Christian calling. I believe, however, that this task is also one of the most challenging and potentially rewarding works in Christian ministry. In this essay I will suggest a range of methodological considerations for the leadership of churches in transitional communities. These methods for ministry are practical and focus upon the leadership role of pastors and ministerial staff in such churches. This statement is intended to stimulate dialogue on the subject and does not pretend to cover all issues involved in serving a transitional community church.

The methods for ministry which I suggest for use in a transitional community church fit into three categories: methods related to your situation, to your strategy, and to yourself.

Methods Related to Your Situation

I suggest three methods for transitional community ministry which are related primarily to the church and community situation of the church: know the territory; stratify your growth goals; and avoid "quick-fix" solutions.

Know the Territory

It is essential for the minister in a transitional community church to have a better-than-average grasp of the facts about his community and church. Too many pastors of changing community churches came to the field without "knowing what they had bought." In some measure, it is almost impossible to know fully what you have gotten yourself into until you arrive on the scene and begin to feel the pulse of the institution. It has been my experience that far more transitional community pastors are disappointed than elated by what they find.

This lack of awareness about the territory usually is not caused by the typical pastor-search committee attempting to obscure the facts, but rather because most committee members—though they are leaders of their churches—do not understand the sociological changes in their community and the implications of those changes for the institutional life of their church. This situation is complicated by the fact that many prospective pastors, considering a move to a church in a transitional community one, did not know what questions to ask in the first place.

Therefore, a wise early course for the transitional community pastor—to be repeated at appropriate intervals during his pastorate—is a careful study of church and community so that goals can be set on the basis of a realistic hope built upon a solid data base. The Southern Baptist Convention offers assistance to its churches through a PACT (Project: Assistance for Churches in Transition) consultation, a thorough church and community study process.

I remember when I set an unrealistic attendance goal for the transitional community church which I served as pastor in the 1970s. Although I had done doctoral study in the field of church and community, I overlooked something relatively obvious in my own parish. Willis Bennett, on a consulting trip to my church field, pointed out to me what should have been obvious! An impartial, uninvolved consultant is often able to see implications of the church and community interaction which escape one more integrally involved in the day-by-day leadership of the church.

The failure of a pastor to set goals on the basis of accurate data can cause unrealistic expectations to arise among the membership. The result is usually an aggravation of the emotional turmoil which both pastor and people feel in many transitional community churches. There is no more cardinal principle for the leadership of the transitional community church than this—the church and its leaders must understand the facts about the community and they must understand the facts about their church organization in order to be able to make useful plans.

Stratify Your Growth Goals

Closely related to the matter of "knowing the territory" is an approach to numerical church growth goals which I believe to be quite adaptable to many transitional community churches. In recent years, I have come more and more to believe that church growth must be openly discussed in transitional community churches. I have recognized in myself the typical transitional community pastor's reluctance to broach this subject at all because we usually come out looking bad in comparison with churches in the growing suburbs. I believe that we must address the church-growth question in transitional community churches. I suggest a method of goal setting which is stratified.

Let me return to the example of the church I served during the 1970s. We had large numbers of senior adults—nearly 60 percent of our Sunday School attendance—and it was absolutely inevitable that the numbers of these persons would decline for several years. This was inevitable because most of the senior adults in that community had a loyalty to some church and would not consider a change. It simply was not possible for the church to replenish its senior adults as fast as they were dying or becoming disabled. The church had few middle-aged adults. Furthermore, because many moved to the suburbs in the early 1970s, there were almost no middle-aged adults in the community—churched or unchurched. Therefore, no reasonable projection could anticipate significant growth in middle adult enrollment. To get more middle adults in the church and community, we had to "grow our own."

But young adults were a different story. There was a ready field for reaching "babyboomers" with small children. In their late twenties and early thirties, they were settling down in our community as first-time home owners. In that strata of the population, we could and did set growth goals which were attained. Our active worshiping and working core of young adults more than doubled, from about thirty to about seventy-five in a few years. Our preschool departments grew, for obvious reasons. When measured in the usual Southern Baptist fashion, we were still a church experiencing a numerical decline because of the senior attrition rate. But I argue that real church growth took place in that situation. I believe it appropriate to stratify our growth goals in the transitional community church on the basis of age and, probably, other sociological factors as well. Although the average attendance dropped, real church growth took place as the congregation built a new foundation underneath that creaky old institution. You will know how to apply the principle to your own situation in order appropriately to stratify your growth goals so that they are specific, attainable, and measurable—with emphasis on the attainable.

Avoid "Quick-Fix" Solutions

One ubiquitous pitfall for the transitional community church is the "simple and easy" solution to all our problems. These proposals come in wide variety. A church may conclude that it can solve its problem of declining numbers by securing the services of a pastor with a strong track record in evangelism. It is certainly important to have a pastor who is a strong evangelist. However, if the church steadfastly refuses to acknowledge the changes that have taken place in its community, or if the church is not willing to reach out to a radically different kind of people who now live in their community, then their solution is a "quick fix" which is doomed to failure because it is inadequate at best and hypocritical at worst.

Other examples of quick fixes abound. One elderly deacon was convinced, for example, that if the deacons would kneel in prayer at the communion table (as they used to do in the "glory days" of the church) for fifteen minutes before the Sunday morning worship service, hordes of people would return to church. A popular "quick fix" in aging churches is the assumption that calling a young pastor brings large numbers of young adults back to church. Watch out for such "quick fixes." They fail because they do not recognize the church and community situation.

Methods Related to Your Strategy

The five methodological considerations which follow deal primarily with matters of leadership strategy. These approaches to ministry are vitally important in the changing community church: balance the prophetic with the pastoral; balance social ministries and evangelism; preach your vision; build upon success; and admit your mistakes.

Balance the Prophetic and the Pastoral

James Glasse has popularized the phrase, "paying the rent," in a local church ministry. There are some routine features of ministry which pastors must fulfill before they will have any latitude to be innovative. If pastors wish to "sell" new approaches to ministry to their churches or bridge some racial or social barrier, they must first faithfully fulfill their flock's expectations in pastoral ministry.

Visiting the sick, preparing well to preach, dropping in on the senior citizens meeting, handling routine organization and administration well—these and many other pastoral functions are necessary ingredients of paying the rent. These must be done before the church will have any tolerance for innovation on the part of its leader. Paying the rent is particularly important with the older membership of the church, among whom the pastor had best be on solid footing before seeking to bring change.

Many transitional community churches need to hear a prophetic word. Many churches are so lethargic that unless the pastor jars the people out of complacency, necessary changes will not transpire. Whether it involves a challenge to spiritual apathy, a condemnation of racism or class prejudice, a critique of the church's preoccupation with internal matters, or other such problems, pastors of transitional community churches may have to be firmly prophetic in order to do what God has called them to do in that place. They are more likely to succeed in the prophetic role if they have paid the rent. They must balance the prophetic word with the kind of pastoral ministry that earns a hearing for the demands of the gospel.

Balance Social Ministries and Evangelism

The New Testament record of the ministry of Jesus indicates that He viewed mankind in wholeness. Every human being is to be seen by God's representatives as a whole person with features that we variously label as spiritual, emotional, social, and physical. The church, to be true to its Lord, must minister with all its available resources to every kind of human need. It is a mistake for any church to lapse into an imbalance between the helping dimensions of the gospel—Christian social ministry, as we call it—and the message dimensions of the gospel—evangelism as we call it. Such an imbalance can be especially damaging to a transitional community church.

Christian social ministry is an essential part of the ministry of the transitional community church, especially the church in a poor community, but I am persuaded that the church which attempts only helping ministries is doomed to failure. The church must also engage in serious, committed efforts to lead the unsaved and unchurched into the fold. Outreach evangelism legitimizes social ministry as social ministry legitimizes outreach evangelism. Jesus did it that way and so must we.

Preach Your Vision

For the transitional community church, the crucial task in that of dreaming again. In all probability it will be the pastor who first dreams a new dream for the church and sees what it can, by God's grace, become. I believe it important for the pastor to preach his vision, holding up before the people his renewed dream for the church.

Some members and, unfortunately, many pastors seem to feel it better to avoid the subject of the church's difficulty. "Better not to hang out our dirty laundry in public" is the apparent rationale for maintaining a pulpit silence on the crippling church and community interaction the church faces. I believe very strongly that the pastor should tell the truth about the church's decline. The people all know it anyway, and they talk about it on the telephone on Monday. The pastor should tell the truth about the church's liabilities, but also paint a picture of the church's assets and possibilities. He should focus on what the church can, under God, become with commitment and dedication and work. It takes some of the sting out of the pervasive anxiety in the downwardly mobile transitional community church if we just tell our people the truth, but also hold up the vision, the new dream.

Plan for and Build upon Success

Sometimes a new pastor in a transitional community church, out of a clear vision for what that church must be doing and out of eagerness to see the work underway, will press too hard too fast for too much too soon. To risk beginning too many new ministries at one time is to risk unnecessary failure. Few congregations are able to begin a half dozen new major efforts all at once. Since the typical transitional community church views itself with something of a negative self-image anyway, the pastor can hardly risk additional unnecessary failures. These will reinforce the image of the church as a dying institution.

It is a far stronger approach for the pastor to choose carefully one or two ministries that can be developed in a successful way and, based on biblical preaching and sound organizational work, lead the church to succeed in that ministry. When success is evident, the pastor should give it a very high profile. The transitional community church urgently needs to be able to see itself as an institution which can accomplish something. It is far easier to start those half-dozen new ministries by phasing them in one or two at a time, with carefully planned intervals between, so that each new ingredient of the pastor's plan for the ministry of the church can be sold to the congregation on the basis of its success in doing the last one. The transitional community church may have failed at some tasks. Unnecessary failures which arise out of too eager an approach to leadership are very destructive. Leading a single success, and then building upon that success is better.

Admit Your Mistakes

Tackling the ministry of the transitional community church is a challenging task for which our educational institutions and our previous experiences have frequently left us unprepared. The seminaries and other churches we have served can hardly be faulted for this, because the world of the declining transitional community church is so entirely foreign to the background of many. We must acknowledge that many of us in transitional community church leadership are involved in on-the-job training. We should admit to our congregations that we don't have all the answers, and admit when we err.

Methods Related to Yourself

The third category of ministry methods for the transitional community church involves the pastor's basic understanding and utilization of himself. My wife, a clinical social worker, has taught me a basic dictum of her profession. As a social worker, *she* is the primary tool she uses in her work, an insight I believe to be applicable to the practice of ministry as well. God has given you *yourself* as a primary tool for the leadership of that transitional community church. But you can't use a tool unless you understand how it works.

I suggest three considerations which involve your self-understanding: understand and prepare for depression; manage pastoral stress effectively; and reconsider before leaving at the end of three years.

Understand and Prepare for Depression

In twenty-three years of involvement with transitional community churches, I have developed the conviction that few if any transitional community pastors escape occasional bouts with depression. Some may choose to call it something else, but most of us know the experience of feeling thoroughly "down" about our situation.

Most of the depression experienced by transitional community pastors is reactive in nature, stemming from our disappointment in the functioning of our churches and the individuals who comprise them. Several techniques are available for the management of depression:

1. Recognize the primary role of anger in depression. Almost all depressed persons have angry feelings about something. The anger has not been dealt with satisfactorily and is "turned in" upon themselves. Successful management is the finding of a way to release and dissipate the anger.

2. Avoid those who oversupport. Inexperienced counselors almost always try to "cheer you up." It is usually impossible to argue a person out of a depression. The person desiring to be helpful will do better to

listen and encourage the depressed person to talk.

3. Recognize the value of purposeful activity. After getting sufficient rest, get busy doing something specific and measurable which will underscore your sense of self-worth.

4. Recognize that depression is often a matter of choice. It is a mistake to describe depression in passive terms instead of active. Depression is not a circumstance which swoops *ex nihilo* upon an unwary victim. Rather, it is often an emotional state of the depressive's own choosing. When we experience depression, we need to be guided, gently and compassionately, to choose another disposition of the anger.

Manage Pastoral Stress Effectively

Much attention is given to the stress which is an inherent and burdensome part of the work of ministry. The pastorate is a difficult and challenging job. In many circumstances, church staff service may be equally stress producing. While all ministers experience stress, I am convinced that there is no more stressful place anywhere in the Lord's service than the transitional community church. There are, I believe, obvious reasons for this.

The average pastor—whether suburban or inner city—is aggravated and frustrated by the nit-picking, carping littleness of some people in every congregation. The inevitable personality conflicts which must be faced and settled always produce anxiety. The typical pastor experiences personal financial stress and a sense of concern about the goldfish bowl existence of his wife and children. Pastors everywhere experience these and other stress-producing features of ministry.

What is different for the transitional community pastor is that many of the compensating "positive strokes" of the suburban church are not part of his situation. A growing Sunday School attendance, a significant number of baptisms and additions, a young, vital, and growing institution with a great deal of pride in itself and a conviction that its best days lie before it—all of these features which compensate many suburban pastors for the stress of their work are not available to the pastor of the downwardly mobile transitional community church.

The life situation of the congregation affects the pastoral stress quotient. When we don't get the good strokes to go along with the bad ones, we will necessarily accumulate stress more rapidly.

A subconscious feature increases stress. We may have convinced ourselves on the intellectual level that all church growth is not measured in terms of numbers. We may know that our particular situation in a troublesome community setting predicates that our successes will have to be different from those traditional numerical ones. Though we have this head knowledge, many transitional community pastors, on the emotional level, have not come to accept it. There are some of our congregations where the pastoral leadership is superb and the church is still smaller this year than it was last. However, few of us have worked through our emotions about the numbers game enough to be able to handle this circumstance without accumulating additional stress.

Recognizing the higher stress quotient of the transitional community situation is extremely important, but it is even more important to do something about it. One solution is a mature, strong, sharing marriage. Another solution is peer group involvement with others who know and understand the situation. Ministers in any setting can profit from the formation of small groups which meet for the purpose of encouraging each other. Especially for those who deal with the added stress of transitional community churches, taking the initiative to form such a support group is a wise investment of time and energy.

Reconsider Before Leaving at the End of Three Years

Lyle Schaller suggests that the best years of many pastorates rarely begin before the fourth year. In transitional community work particularly, there is a distressing frequency with which our pastors move to the scene with a lot of hope, grapple unsuccessfully—in their minds at least—with the problems for two or three years, and move on to another field of service. Generalizations must be viewed with suspicion, of course, but a premature move before the pastor's best years of service may well be destructive both to the church and to the minister.

As Schaller suggests, attempt to evaluate the passage of time not only in years but also in terms of chapters of ministry. A chapter in ministry may involve months or years, but is measured in terms of significant development in the life of the church, new approaches to ministry attempted, new patterns of relationships built. If you are considering moving from a declining community church after a brief pastorate of perhaps two or three years, try to evaluate what has transpired during that period in terms of chapters. It may be that you have passed through only your introductory chapter. It is, of course, possible that many significant chapters may have transpired during the same period of time. The important insight is to look at more than the number of years served in that place.

Compared to the usual track record of a large number of Southern Baptist ministers, a general principle is that longer is better and that many, many moves after only three years are premature. A great many ministers who present themselves as having had fifteen years experience have really only had three years' experience five different times.

Conclusion

This statement of methodological concerns for the pastoral leadership of transitional community churches is intended to assist the transitional community ministers in evaluating their role in their place of service. There is no easy way to lead a transitional community church. Each of us understands the cry of Paul and Barnabas who resisted the attempt by the Lycaonians to treat them as divine. Each of us echoes their cry, "We also are men, of like nature with you" (Acts 14:15, RSV). We also are flawed mortals who know hurt and struggle as much as do the dedicated lay persons in our churches.

In *The Wounded Healer*, Henri Nouwen recites an old legend in the Jewish Talmud which describes an imaginary encounter between a rabbi and the prophet Elijah. Rabbi Yoshua ben Levi came upon Elijah the prophet standing at the entrance to a cave. He asked Elijah the popular Jewish question, "When will Messiah come?" Elijah replied, "Go and ask Him yourself." "Where is He?" "Sitting at the gates of the city." "How shall I know Him?" "He is sitting among the poor, covered with wounds. The others unbind all their wounds at the same time and then bind them up again. But He unbinds one at a time and binds it up again, saying to himself, 'Perhaps I shall be needed: if so, I must always be ready so as not to delay for a moment.' "

In this old legend, the expected Messiah is pictured as Himself wounded, but with His own wounds so in control that they do not prevent His being able to help others. How much that ancient imaginative story fits the image of Jesus, whom Isaiah described as "wounded for our transgressions" (Isa. 53:5).

We who seek to minister by serving transitional community churches are wounded ministers seeking to lead wounded congregations. But Messiah Himself is a wounded healer.

Notes

1. Jere Allen and George Bullard, *Shaping a Future for the Church in the Changing Community* (Atlanta: Home Mission Board, SBC, 1981). Contact the Metropolitan Missions Department, Home Mission Board, SBC for information. For a list of certified PACT consultants, contact the director of missions for the Southern Baptist state convention serving your area.

2. James D. Glasse, *Putting It Together in the Parish* (Nashville: Abingdon Press, 1972), 53ff.

3. Robert D. Dale, *To Dream Again* (Nashville: Broadman Press, 1981).

4. Lyle E. Schaller, *Survival Tactics in the Parish* (Nashville: Abingdon Press, 1977), 27.

5. Ibid.

6. Henri J. M. Nouwen, *The Wounded Healer* (Garden City, New York: Doubleday and Company, Inc., 1972), 83-84.

||| 8 |||

Moving the Church Off the Plateau

by Jere Allen and Kirk Hadaway

The norm among Southern Baptist churches is to be on the plateau. As we enter the 1990s, 52 percent are on the plateau—defined as growing no more than 10 percent nor declining more than 10 percent in membership within the past five years. This compares to 18 percent that have declined more than 10 percent in membership and 30.5 percent that have grown more than 10 percent within the past five-year period.[1] Because 19,000-plus SBC churches are on the plateau it is critical that church growth efforts be focused on revitalizing these congregations.

Reasons for Plateau

Among many reasons that contribute to churches being on the plateau, two uncontrollable ones are *age* and *context*.[2] Research shows a fifteen-year "growth window" after the birth of a church and a subsequent slowdown. The older the church, the more likely it will be plateaued; and the younger the church, the more likely it will be growing.

Among churches organized prior to 1927 only 25 percent grew by more than 10 percent between 1981 and 1986. The average rate of growth for these older churches was 4 percent. By contrast, 68 percent of churches organized between 1972 and 1981 had a growth rate of 10 percent or higher for the five-year-period. The average rate of growth was 47 percent.[3]

A second uncontrollable factor is *context*—the location of the church's facility. In older, more densely populated areas, where there

is greater pluralism, transition, and poverty, there are often more plateaued churches. In newer suburban and exurban areas where there
are a greater proportion of children, home owners, newer single-fam-
ily houses, and population growth, there are more growing churches.

A study of 114 Southern Baptist churches in Memphis, Tennessee,
showed significant correlation between context and church growth.
Generally, the further the church was located from the central business district, the greater the growth; the closer the church to the central business district, the greater the plateau or decline.[4]

Research on the Plateaued Church

Research has been sparse on the factors that characterize churches
that begin to grow after a significant period of stability. Church-
growth studies have tended to focus on factors that characterize growing churches, but not on what caused the growth to take place. Characteristics that are shared by growing churches are not necessarily
those which caused them to grow, especially when it can be shown
that nongrowing churches have many of the same characteristics.

Two research projects form the basis for this chapter. The first was
conducted in 1983.[5] Letters were written to fifty randomly selected
associational directors of missions with two questions: "Tell why
some churches have been able to come off the plateau" and "Give the
name of a pastor whose church has come off the plateau." A follow-up
letter was written to the pastors surfaced with two questions: "Why
did your director of missions choose your church?" and "Why do you
believe your church came off the plateau? Do not be modest." The
thirty replies from the pastors and thirty-six replies from the directors
of missions were reproduced and used in two separate conferences,
each with approximately fifty associational directors of missions. In
small groups in the first conference, participants were asked to read all
sixty-six letters and from them list reasons why these churches came
off the plateau. The small-group lists were then correlated by all in the
conference into one list of nine factors. The same process was used in a
second conference the following month with fifty directors of mis-

sions. When the small-group lists were combined for this second group, the surprise was they had the same factors listed as the first group and the first four were in identical order.

The nine factors that surfaced for moving a church off the plateau were as follows: (1) Pastoral leadership; (2) Attitudinal change, especially in regard to growth; (3) Revitalization of existing programs, especially the Sunday School; (4) Awareness and responsiveness to "people needs" in the community; (5) Spiritual renewal through prayer and Holy Spirit; (6) Planning/goal setting; (7) Training and utilization of present and new leadership; (8) Evangelistic outreach and visitation; (9) Atmosphere of love/unity/fellowship.

The second research project was conducted in 1988.[6] Churches were selected which had been on statistical plateaus from 1978 through 1983. The list contained churches which neither gained nor lost more than 5 percent in total membership during that five-year period nor 5 percent in any one of the years. These churches were undoubtedly on the plateau.

From this list two groups were selected based on their total membership and average Sunday School attendance for 1983 through 1986. The first group was composed of churches that continued to stay on the plateau during this second period. They were called "continued plateaued churches."

The second group included churches that had been plateaued 1978 through 1983 but had then grown 15 percent or more both in total membership and Sunday School average attendance 1983 to 1986. They were called "breakout churches."

An eight-page questionnaire containing eighty-eight closed-ended questions (many with multiple choices) and four open-ended questions was mailed in the spring of 1988 to both groups. Returns provided 184 usable questionnaires, roughly divided between the continued plateaued churches and breakout churches.

Significant factors that emerged from the data collected were placed in the following categories: (1) The pastor; (2) Openness to change; (3) Planning and goal setting; (4) Revitalization of programs (outreach and assimilation; Sunday School; worship; ministry; training and other programs); (5) Congregational renewal; (6) Facilities and the church setting.

This chapter will combine the findings of the two research reports on the church on the plateau, along with interviews conducted in plateaued churches and the writings of others.

The Pastor and a Vision for Growth

The pastor and a vision for growth are linked together as perhaps the two most important factors in moving the church off the plateau. Though a vision for growth by laypersons may precede that of the pastor, the potential for growth will not be fully realized without the pastor's catching and promoting that vision.

1. Pastoral leadership.—In a growing church, bold and active leadership is not as necessary as in a plateaued church. To produce a turnaround, the pastor must be a change agent. This necessarily involves unfreezing the present situation, moving the group to a new level and refreezing the group life at the new level. Kennon Callahan in *Twelve Keys to an Effective Church* writes:

> The time for leaders has come, the time for enablers has passed....
> Whenever the concept of enabler has been linked with nondirective counseling techniques, the local church has suffered from dysfunctional leadership. The reactive, responsive, process-centered style of leadership present in many local congregations contributes significantly to those congregations being declining or dying congregations. . . . In no sense am I advocating that leaders should become dictatorial and authoritarian. . . . I am strongly against those who see themselves as enablers whenever they use their enabler philosophy as a cop-out to avoid sharing their own agenda, direction, and vision straightforwardly.[7]

A pastor who had led his church off the plateau wrote: "The catalyst for growth is rooted in the aggressive leadership I have given to the church." A director of missions suggested: "If a church is to come off the plateau, then it must have strong, vigorous pastoral leadership."

Richard G. Hutcheson, Jr., in *Wheel Within the Wheel: Confronting the Management Crisis of the Pluralistic Church* defines the enabler role as "a relatively uninvolved technician who understands the process by which things are accomplished, and who enables others to achieve goals."[8] He traces the enabler role back to the group dynamics work of Kurt Lewin, which stressed interpersonal relationships. Power, aggressive leadership, and control were looked down upon, with the desire that decisions be made through consensus.

Lyle Schaller has suggested that the "pastor as enabler" model reached its peak of popularity in the late 1960s and has been declining since then. In *Growing Plans* Schaller declared: "The greater the lay control in any size congregation, the less likely it is that the congregation will begin and maintain significant numerical growth."[9]

This is not a call for an autocratic leader. That style is counterproductive to leading a church off the plateau and will, in the long run, fail. Nor is this a call for an enabler, *when it is defined as above*. The need is for pastors who are strong visionary leaders.

The importance of the pastor in breakout churches was underscored in findings on how long the present pastor had served. Forty-three percent of the breakout churches had their present pastors four to six years; this contrasts with less than 7 percent for the continued plateaued churches. A follow-up study of the Uniform Church Letter for 1983 showed that 59 percent of the breakout churches had called pastors in 1982 or 1983, the last year of the plateau. Apparently, a new pastor is often necessary to revitalize a stagnant church; if a church is going to follow the leadership of its pastor off the plateau, the change usually occurs soon after the start of ministry.

Schaller wrote,

Most of the long-tenure members lack the skills, the time, the desire, the authority, or the energy to initiate a strategy for change. Therefore, the likeliest candidate to initiate this strategy is the just-arrived "new minister," who possess the freedom of the outsider, still has some discretionary time in every month, holds the authority that goes with the office of pastor, has no stake in maintaining the status quo, possesses a strong evangelistic concern, and has gifts and skills in the process of planned change.[10]

Is it necessary to be a new pastor of a church to lead it off the plateau? The answer is no. Research shows that 22 percent of breakout churches had the same pastor both during the period of plateau and significant growth. There are excellent examples of pastors who have changed their style from business as usual to a determination to be proactive and make a profound difference in the growth pattern of the church. Often this change has followed a sabbatical leave, a fresh study of the meaning and purpose of the church, an action-reflection trip to study growing churches, a significant retreat away from the church field, or a personal crisis. In other cases there has been a change in makeup or attitude of the lay leadership, allowing the pastor the proper role of visionary leader.

Factors related to the pastor's style that were characteristic of the breakout church pastor, but not as strong in some pastors of the continued plateaued church were: having "vision"; holding a conservative view of the Bible; being evangelistic, hardworking, people-oriented, caring, and goal-directed; delivering more challenging as opposed to comforting sermons; visiting more prospects on average; and being somewhat less patient.

Traits that were not significantly different in pastors of plateaued and breakout churches and are thereby apparently unrelated to breakout growth are: a seminary education, an authoritarian leadership style, rating themselves as better administrators or as preaching sermons which are more bold, clear, exciting or practical than pastors of churches still on the plateau.

2. A Vision for growth.—This factor includes attitude, morale, and sense of direction. When a vision to reach out to the unchurched and lost permeates the membership and especially the leadership, the church is on its way to a turnaround. The pastor as visionary leader plays a pivotal role in this factor.

G. W. Garvin wrote, "Churches grow that 'articulate a distinct and winsome identity.' They develop a 'unifying vision.' Developing this vision is the primary task for leadership of these growing congregations. The task falls primarily on the shoulders of the minister who is head of staff and secondarily on the leadership core of the congregation."[11]

Forty-six percent of the breakout churches are very excited (as opposed to apathetic), in comparison to 19 percent of churches continuing on the plateau. The pastor who is able to generate enthusiasm is the one most likely to move a church off the plateau.

A layperson in a church that had come off of a lengthy plateau in a significant way wrote: "Our pastor's enthusiasm just naturally sparks enthusiasm." Others said, "It has been the result of an enthusiastic pastor who does everything with a gusto of enthusiasm which is contagious and spreads like a prairie fire among our people," and "Our pastor loves the Lord with all his heart and has so much enthusiasm that it just grabs everyone around him." Fire does beget fire.

The following are some ways a pastor can ignite enthusiasm for growth: (1) Expose members on field trips to enthusiastic, growing churches that were formerly on the plateau; (2) Take leaders on a retreat away from the church facility for prayer and in-depth study of the mission and purpose of the church; (3) Use an enthusiastic outside consultant to lead the church through a planning process; (4) Publicize victories before the church; accentuate the positive things that are happening; (5) Lead the members to set specific and attainable growth goals and reward them through public recognition for accomplishments; (6) Lead members to study individually and in small groups church-growth books, especially those heavy on models of success; and (7) Share growth dreams with the congregation.

Truly, "Without a vision, the people perish." A church needs a clear and simple biblically-based vision toward which all the other dreams lead. It needs to be specific, repeated often, and capable of being articulated by the average church member.

Organizational Development

A unified vision needs to be supplemented with strategic planning, effective outreach efforts, and revitalization of the church program structures. A dream without planning is as ineffective as planning without a dream. Dreaming and planning must go hand-in-hand. Ideally, the dream precedes the plan, but often a unified dream comes during the planning process.

3. Planning and goal setting.—"Strategic planning is the process by which an organization envisions its future and develops the necessary procedures and operations to achieve that future."[12]

Churches on the plateau tend toward continuity rather than intentional change. They drift aimlessly with little internal guidance. Even though they are busy doing many good things they are not engaged in the essentials for growth. Forty percent of breakout churches have a long-range plan in place, compared to 18 percent of the continued plateaued churches.

One of the strongest correlations of breakout growth was the increased emphasis on goal setting. Sixty-four percent of the breakout churches, and only 26 percent in the continued plateaued churches had this increased emphasis. This was no real surprise. Churches on the plateau are typically in a maintenance mode, allowing the past ways of doing things to dictate the present and future. What they need is change, and planning can help in this. Charles Chaney and Ron Lewis wrote, "Some churches do not plan at all. Whatever happens just happens and no definite course of action is followed."[13]

Numerical goal-setting is important. In a 1984 Home Mission Board study contrasting the fastest-growing and typical Southern Baptist Convention churches, one of the summary observations was, "Numerical growth is receiving priority in the fastest growing churches to a greater degree than the typical churches . . . the fastest-growing churches do think more about numbers."[14] In the 1988 Church on the Plateau Research Project, 65 percent of the breakout churches set membership goals, where only 36 percent of continued plateaued churches did so.

Therefore, planning and goal-setting should be a high priority for moving a church off the plateau. In strategic planning, churches go through the following steps:

(1) Pastor leads the church to struggle through a statement on its reason for being; (2) Church study committee gathers objective and subjective data on the church and its community; (3) Cross section of leadership sets a few priority or goal areas that grow out of their purpose and church and community situation, and present to the church specific, attainable, and measurable goals that serve as a measuring stick for the success of a strategic plan; (4) Church Council sets action plans with activities, persons responsible, dates for accomplishment, and resources needed.

In church strategic planning, it is necessary to involve as many church members as possible. The old adage, "No one is lazier than the person in pursuit of someone else's goals," leads to an equally valid adage, "No one exerts as much energy as the person in pursuit of his/her own goals." Roger H. Waterman, Jr., in *The Renewal Factor*, says, "The renewing companies recognize the value of the planning process even though they don't believe it generates their companies' major strategies."[15] He sees the value in the process itself because it provides "opportunity generation, with a good dose of communication thrown in as well."[16] Also, it brings people closer together. " 'The importance of planning is the *process*,' people often say, and then go on to explain that the plans themselves don't appear to matter as much as the fact that they have a planning process."[17]

This is not to depreciate the value of the plan produced, but to accentuate the importance of ownership, input, and communication that takes place when laypersons are allowed to develop a long-range plan for a church.

4. Revitalization of the church programs, especially the Sunday School.—After a poor Saturday performance, the football coach announced to the team, "On Monday we're back to the basics." That is excellent advice for the church on the plateau. Before taking off on the latest fad or fiddling with the newest gimmick for raising attendance, a church should rebuild its infrastructure. There is little point in starting an aggressive visitation program for Sunday School when the groupings, facilities, and leadership training are not in place.

Though all the programs of the church may need revitalization, this section gives major emphasis to the Sunday School because research shows breakout churches tend to have better functioning Sunday Schools than churches which remain on the plateau. While pastor of First Baptist Church in Shreveport, Louisiana, Bill Hull preached on "The Cruciality of the Sunday School."

> I have come to a deep and abiding conviction that the missing ingredient so essential to our fulfillment as a church is a vital growing Sunday School. . . . Based on Biblical, theological, and practical necessities, I have concluded that the Sunday School is not an option but an imperative. As John Sisemore has insisted, the Sunday School is not just one aspect or feature or program of the church but is the church organized to fulfill the Great Commission.[18]

This is the message the leadership of the church on the plateau needs to proclaim.

Clearly and simply the way to revitalize the Sunday School is what is commonly called "Flake's Formula." These principles are the key to Andy Anderson's *Growth Spiral* and are central to much of what is now taught as Church Growth.

Building a Standard Sunday School by Arthur Flake gives the following for meeting the Standard of Excellence:

(1) *The Constitution for the Sunday School should be known.*— He suggests studying the church membership roll and taking a "religious census" or "house-to-house canvass."

(2) *The organization should be enlarged.*—This is necessary to take care of all the people that will be discovered in the census (note the confidence building). A part of this point is a training class for the new teachers.

(3) *A suitable place should be provided.*—This includes adequate

and well-equipped meeting rooms.

(4) *The enlarged organization should be inaugurated.*—This includes proper grading, use of the six-point record system, assignment of classes, and the giving of prospective students to the teacher.

(5) *A program of visitation should be maintained.*—He pleads for all teachers to visit every prospective student the following week and then keep visiting them from week to week with the same urgent invitation until all of them join. Thereafter, he urges a monthly visitation program for absentees, prospects, and newcomers.[19]

A key principle in moving a church off the plateau is adding new units. Kennon Callahan in *Twelve Keys to an Effective Church* wrote:

> It should be observed that new people tend to join new groups....
> new people in a church tend to search out new groups in which they can
> establish relationships of sharing and caring. The reason for this is very
> simple. It is easier for new people to establish deeply profound relation-
> ships with one another when the network of relationships is still com-
> paratively new, flexible, and in process for development. . . . As open
> and as genuinely caring as that old group seeks to be, it nevertheless
> takes new people a good deal of time to learn and discover their place in
> that already fully established network of relationships. . . . Those
> churches that quit starting new groups are churches that have decided
> to die.[20]

Churches moving off the plateau are starting new units by recruiting teachers and outreach leaders and handing them fresh prospect lists. The pastor and church leaders give blocks of time to equipping, sending out, supporting, calling to accountability and recognizing these allies who are creating new units.

Only half of the churches which continued on the plateau began new classes in the past year, as compared to 70 percent of the breakout churches.

One of the strongest differences between breakout and plateaued churches in all categories was the children's Sunday School. They both had a "good" children's Sunday School, but 22 percent of the breakout churches had exceptional ones compared to 5 percent of those continuing on the plateau.

Other differences that were significantly better in the breakout churches were: a better adult, singles, and youth program, better nurseries; more acceptance of newcomers; and more likelihood of having a Sunday School workers training class.

Areas that were not significantly different, and thereby not likely to be related to moving a church off the plateau were: weekly workers' meetings, Sunday School outreach leaders, and a pastor's class.

5. Evangelistic outreach and visitation.—By far, the greatest contrast between breakout and plateaued churches was in evangelistic outreach and visitation. On a question regarding "winning the lost, evangelism," 54 percent of the breakout churches rated themselves as exceptional or good, compared to 4 percent of the plateaued churches. On a continuum from 1 to 9, with 1 being totally unevangelistic and 9 being evangelistic, 65 percent of the pastors of breakout churches scored it 7 to 9, as compared to 26 percent for plateaued churches. Questions which dealt with "recruitment or outreach" did not show as wide a contrast as those that dealt with "evangelism" and "winning the lost."

Breakout churches report that considerably more of their additions have come from conversion of the unchurched and a smaller percent from baptizing the children of members. Breakout churches are also reaching a higher proportion of persons age thirty to forty-four, an age group which tends to have more younger children.

Though research shows strong contrasts in evangelistic *emphasis,* the contrast in *specific techniques* is not as strong. In order of importance, breakout churches are more likely to have weekly visitation programs, maintain active prospect files, conduct a religious census in their geographical areas, provide a regular evangelism training program, and send a mass mailout to community residents.

Visitation of prospects is obviously stronger in breakout churches. Seventy-one percent of breakout churches conduct visitation at least weekly compared to 43 percent of plateaued churches. Most churches do visitation, but the contrast is in its purpose. In breakout churches, visitation is more likely to be for evangelism and winning the lost.

A visitation program in and of itself will not bring about growth. It must be linked to a growth attitude that permeates the congregation. Visits to breakout churches reveal a spirit of growth that permeates worship services, Sunday School, and all aspects of the church program.

Undergirding Factors

The remaining three factors should not be thought of as "in order." These undergird the factors above. For example, "Spiritual renewal through the Holy Spirit and prayer" would not only precede all the factors above but would be prevalent in all of them.

6. *Awareness of and responsiveness to people needs.*—In the 1983 survey this ranked as the fourth characteristic of churches that had come off the plateau. In Callahan's *Twelve Keys to an Effective Church* "specific, concrete missional objectives" is the first key.

The term "meeting people needs" showed up in numerous letters from churches on the plateau in different parts of the nation, even though that term is not common in the SBC denominational glossary. The denomination prefers Christian social ministry, mission action, and mission ministries. In both conferences, where the directors of missions studied the letters "people needs" surfaced in terminology.

In the 1988 research there was significant contrast between the breakout and continued plateaued churches on the question: "How involved is your church in providing ministry to the surrounding community?" The breakout church pastors said 37 percent of their churches were doing so "to a large extent" and a total of 92 percent were doing so "to some or a large extent." This is in contrast to the 17 percent of the plateaued churches who were doing so to a large extent and 75 percent to some or a large extent. Breakout churches were also more likely to conduct specialized ministries, to have given increased emphasis to ministry to the community during the past several years and to have "a desire to minister."

Rather than evangelism and ministry working against one another, they were shown to be complementary as churches came off the plateau. Breakout churches appear to be less inward looking and to see the role of the church as helping persons in their time of need. As a result, persons in the community become aware that the church exists and is available when they face crises in their lives. When a church begins to meet needs, the community grapevine labels that congregation as a caring group of people.

The goal of providing ministry to the community is not to produce church growth, but to meet needs; the new being in Christ sends the church forth as a caring body. Ministry is not a handmaiden for evangelism; the church body does not provide for others based on the growth potential due to the ones helped. However, evangelistic growth often results as a serendipity of caring. Often relationships are established between church and community that results in the spiritual as well as the material needs being met.

7. Spiritual renewal through the Holy Spirit and prayer.—Growing churches may be falsely accused of sacrificing spiritual maturity for pragmatism and an overemphasis on numbers. This may be true in isolated cases, but in general, research shows the breakout churches say they are giving greater emphasis to prayer and growing in the faith than in plateaued churches. Sixty-four percent of the breakout churches say the "spiritual growth of members" is either exceptional or good as compared to 34 percent of the plateaued churches. Prayer has received an increased emphasis in 70 percent of the breakout churches in the past several years, compared to 40 percent of the plateaued churches.

This renewed spirit is evident in the worship services as well; seventy-six percent of breakout churches indicated a spirit of celebration as compared to 47 percent of plateaued churches. Inspiration was evident in 92 percent of the breakout churches and 70 percent of the plateaued churches.

It appears a new vision, evangelism, social ministry, and spiritual growth all are perceived by pastors of breakout churches as rising together.

This is not to suggest that there is not equal Christian commitment in the plateaued church. Lyle Schaller insisted strongly,

> Notice must be taken of those who allege that the primary reason any congregation fails to grow, regardless of size, is the lack of Christian commitment among the members. This is nonsense! . . . I have found no evidence to suggest that the commitment to Jesus Christ as Lord and Savior is any less among the members of the small-membership churches than it is among the members of rapidly-growing churches. There may be a difference in how members of different churches *express* their Christian commitment, but that is a different subject from the *depth* of commitment.[21]

Schaller further declared, "The small church tends to focus on nurture, not mission."[22] He said others suggest small churches are "too inward-oriented and most of the limited resources are concentrated on serving the members and on institutional survival."[23]

It should not be implied that the *depth* of commitment of breakout churches is higher, but the *expression* of commitment appears to be focused on the community outside of the membership. Also, research shows the outward expression of their faith is more enthusiastic, joyful, celebrative, expectant, inspirational and spontaneous.

8. Training and utilization of present and new leadership.—Churches in a numerical rut often choose nominating committees consisting of long-term older members who nominate those who have been faithful through the years. Churches that begin to grow include newer, more creative, and younger members on the nominating committee.

Things which are new bring churches off the plateau: a new or renewed pastor, new vision, new units, and new leaders. There must be change in the direction of growth rather than sameness in the rut of stability.

Research shows that the breakout churches gave an increased emphasis on the training of lay leaders. Fifty-six percent of breakout churches reported an increase in lay leader training within the last several years as compared to 36 percent of the plateaued churches.

Pastors cannot produce growth alone. Though they must be visionary leaders and be accepted by the church leaders, they cannot make churches grow without sharing leadership with laity. Carl Dudley said that pastors can set the vision for a church, but the laypersons must institutionalize that vision. Well said!

In one church that has come off the plateau, new Sunday school units are continually being formed. They are constantly in a building program to create more room. Therefore, new Sunday School teachers are needed throughout the year. This church has a one-hour introductory course on becoming a Sunday School teacher that is held during the Sunday School hour. Participants are immediately assigned for on-the-job training to the age-group class where they will eventually teach. They are required to attend a nine-month course of study with three months each in the following classes: (1) How to Study the Bible, (2) What Do Baptists Believe? and (3) How to Share Your Faith. On one Sunday, this church began sixty-four new Sunday School units.

Conclusion

A community develops and soon afterward its residents form a church. As the community grows, the church grows. Then, as the community stabilizes so does the church. There are minor ups and downs, but the attendance stays steady year by year. Is this satisfactory? Should not the church grow when 44 percent of the (typical) church community is unchurched?[24]

Notes

1. C. Kirk Hadaway, "Growing Off the Plateau: A Summary of the 1988 'Church on the Plateau' Survey" (Nashville: Research Services Department, Sunday School Board of the SBC, February 1989), 1. Material from this study is used extensively in this chapter.

2. W. Jere Allen, "Helping the Church on the Plateau," in *Associational Bulletin* (Atlanta: Associational Missions Division, Home Mission Board of the SBC, January/ February 1989), vol. 23, no. 1, 1-2. Material from this article is used throughout this

chapter.

3. C. Kirk Hadaway, "New Churches and Church Growth in the Southern Baptist Convention" (Nashville: Research Services Department, Sunday School Board of the SBC, November 1987), 1-2.

4. C. Kirk Hadaway, "Church Growth (and Decline) in a Southern City" in *Review and Religious Research* 23 (June 1982): 376.

5. Jere Allen, "Church on the Plateau Research Project" in *Church on the Plateau* (Atlanta: Home Mission Board of the SBC, unpublished document, 1984), 51-56.

6. Hadaway, "Growing Off the Plateau."

7. Kennon L. Callahan, *Twelve Keys to an Effective Church* (San Francisco: Harper and Row, 1983), 41-42.

8. Richard G. Hutcheson, Jr., *Wheel Within the Wheel: Confronting the Management Crisis of the Pluralistic Church* (Atlanta: John Knox Press, 1979), 54.

9. Lyle E. Schaller, *Growing Plans* (Nashville: Abingdon Press, 1984), 18.

10. Ibid., 23.

11. G. W. Garvin, "Marks of Growing Churches" in "Action Information" (Washington, D.C.: Alban Institute, August-September 1985), vol. XI, no. 5, 2.

12. J. William Pfeiffer, "Applied Strategic Planning: A New model for Organizational Growth and Vitality in *Strategic Planning* (San Diego: University Association, 1986), 2.

13. Charles L. Chaney and Ron S. Lewis, *Design for Church Growth* (Nashville: Broadman Press, 1978), 34.

14. David B. Jones and Phillip B. Jones, "Abstract of a Study of Fastest Growing Churches in the Southern Baptist Convention 1975 to 1980" (Atlanta: Planning and Services Research Department, Home Mission Board, SBC, July 1984), 3.

15. Roger H. Waterman, Jr., *The Renewal Factor* (New York: Bantam Books, 1987), 49.

16. Ibid.

17. Ibid., 52.

18. William E. Hull, "The Cruciality of the Sunday School" in *Shreveport Sermons* (Shreveport, La: The First Baptist Church in Shreveport, preached October 1, 1978), 1 and 3.

19. Arthur Flake, *Building a Standard Sunday School* (Nashville: Convention Press, 1922, revised 1928), 25-39.

20. Callahan, 36-37.

21. Schaller, 21.

22. Ibid., 19.

23. Ibid.

24. "The Unchurched American—10 Years Later" (Princeton, N.J.: The Princeton Research Center, 1988), 2.

9

Confronting Ethical Issues

by W. David Sapp

Pollster: Well, Amos, I have been over the draft of this prophecy you're working on, and I want to suggest a few changes for your consideration.

Amos: Oh, really? What changes would you suggest?

Pollster: Well, there are just a few things. I realize you are a man of convictions, but I also know you really want this book to sell. I mean, how much can you influence people with your convictions if the book doesn't sell?

Amos: I see your point.

Pollster: Take this line about folks who sell the righteous for silver and the needy for a pair of shoes. I'm really worried that you might offend some people there.

Amos: Well, sure, but . . . .

Pollster: Lots of people don't care much for the righteous or the needy. You know how uppity those Pharisees can get. And there are beggars all over on the streets of Jerusalem who ought to be out working for a living.

Amos: Any other suggestions?

Pollster: Well, here where you have God saying "I slew your young men with the sword." Some folks are going to think you are making God out to be a barbarian.

Amos: But that's what He said!

Pollster: Now, don't get touchy. I was just trying to be helpful.

Amos: But God told me to say those things! I don't have any choice.

Pollster: But if you want to have any influence, you must stay away from divisive subjects!

Amos: I'm sorry, I wish I could take your advice, but there is one more thing God said: "For three transgressions of pollsters and for four, I will not revoke the punishment."

Confronting ethical issues is an essential, if not easy, part of Christian ministry. The pollsters may encourage avoidance, but neither the Bible nor the culture will allow the church to ignore issues. The Scripture is shot through with demands for involvement, and the culture comes up with a new issue nearly every day for which it looks to the church for insight, if not guidance. The biblical prophet Amos understood this well.

These issues come in many forms: racial problems, family stress, substance abuse, crime, child molestation, spouse abuse, starvation, and a host of others. To confront these problems requires supreme courage and delicate judgment. It requires the courage of Amos and the wisdom of Solomon. It requires ministers who listen to the voice of God before the advice of the pollsters and who sincerely believe that the kingdom of God is more important than all the kingdoms of this world.

In this chapter I will speak primarily of the function of the professional minister in confronting issues, but of course the task belongs to the whole church. A few practical observations, however, may be of special help to ministers as they lead the church.[1]

1. *The biblical task of the minister requires the deliberate development of an ethical consciousness.*—A part of the calling of the minister is a calling to prophetic ministry. "Warn my people of their sins!" says the Scripture. Every minister serves to some degree as a moral guide for church and society. If he fails to do this then he has failed in his biblical calling.

To serve this function well requires enormous conviction and inner strength. The pressures of any community toward conformity in ethical judgments is nearly irresistible, and the risk of resisting that pressure is tremendous. If prophets are to be raised up in God's churches, there must be ministers who have developed a sharply focused, divinely informed ethical sensitivity.

How is such a sensitivity developed? A highly developed sensitivity to ethical issues is *not* automatic in all believers. If it were, whole sections of the Bible could have been omitted. What need would there be for the Ten Commandments, for most of the prophets, or for the Sermon on the Mount? For most of us, ethical sensitivity must be cultivated.

While some may find it surprising, I believe that the primary arena in which a strong ethical consciousness is developed is the devotional life. This really should not surprise anyone. Those who are intimately involved with the God of love and justice should be driven toward the practice of love and justice in the world He created.

A strong devotional orientation begins with a serious involvement with the Bible. I once thought that the way to be involved with the Bible was to see it as a kind of law book or cookbook or repair manual. When you wanted to know the right things to do, you simply consulted the right rule in the Book. When you needed a recipe for a zestier life, you found the appropriate biblical instruction and cooked up a new life. When something was broken in your life, you went to the Bible to find out how to repair the damage. This approach was fine as far as it went, but it did not go far enough. In fact, it allowed me to develop some profound misinterpretations of Scripture, and it was certainly inadequate for a life of ministry.

Later I discovered that the Bible is far more than a reference book. It is a living document of love. It is as far above a reference book as Shakespeare is above a cookbook. No, on second thought, it is even further. Our Bible is a love letter from God and it will shape our confrontation with every ethical issue if we bathe our souls in its teaching.

If the Bible is to be a helpful ethical resource for the minister, he must know it both through critical scholarship and devotional involvement. He must know the Bible through the eyes of the scholar in order to understand the ethical teaching of the Bible in its original setting. (Errors here are accountable for much of the worst theology we perpetrate on unsuspecting Christians.) Furthermore, he needs the objectivity of the scholar if he is able to hear what the Bible is saying without reading his own prejudice into the text.

Even more important than reading the Bible with scholarly understanding, he must read it with devotional understanding. He must be a lover of the Scripture who spends tender hours letting the love of God, the primary ethical principle, address him through Holy Writ. One of the ways in which I have sought to do this is through keeping a journal of interaction with the Scripture. As I read, I write reactions, questions, fears, joys, tears, and victories. Among other things, I endeavor to let the Bible make me more aware of wrong in the world and more aware of God's standards of righteousness. I try to allow the Bible to correct both my understanding and my behavior.

Another technique used by many, and too often neglected nowadays, is memorization. It is hard to commit the words of the Bible to memory without allowing them to deepen our ethical sensitivities.

The Bible itself has a phrase which tells us what this devotional approach to Scripture does for those who would apply the faith to life. The psalmist spoke again and again of his "delight in the law of the Lord." Only one who has learned to delight in the law of the Lord rather than in the praise of mankind can find the courage necessary for the confrontation of sin.

Another area of the devotional life which feeds an ethical consciousness is prayer. Of course, prayer provides strength for ethical confrontation, but equally important, prayer informs the ethical judgments of the minister. Prayer allows the Holy Spirit to teach the minister the ways of God. As P. T. Forsythe once said, "Prayer is to religion what original research is to science."[2]

The importance of prayer as a source of ethical strength and wisdom should be obvious. Yet many people see prayer as a retreat from the world, as a disengagement from the arena of action. This is a false understanding. In the first place, prayer *is* action. To pray is to do something. To pray is change things. In the second place, prayer is active preparation for other kinds of action. Real prayer does not leave one pensively in the cloister, but drives one actively into the world. The wilderness was always a place of retreat for Jesus, but it was never a place to live. Prayer provides both motivation and information for ministers who work to kindle the flame of righteousness.

While these two suggestions for developing an ethical consciousness have to do with the spiritual arena, the true prophet must also be involved in the secular arena. Prayer and Bible study can be reduced to escapism if we fail to pray over the newspaper and apply the teachings of the Bible to the events of our day.

A prophet must know what is going on in the world. If he is to deliver God's message to the king, he must know what the king is doing. A Nathan cannot stand before a David if he is ignorant of the secular world. In this sense at least, we must have a worldly ministry if we are ever to have a godly world.

2. *The minister needs judgment in dealing with ethical issues.*—The minister must know when to speak and when to be silent, when to encourage and when to chide, when to address an issue and when to let it lie. He must develop enough courage to be a martyr if necessary and enough wisdom not to be martyred in vain.

My own observation is that judgment is not a quality which can be learned. When interviewing a prospective church staff member on one occasion, I had questions about the young man's judgment and consulted a trusted adviser for help. "If he has judgment the day you call him," counseled my friend, "he'll have judgment the day he resigns. If he doesn't have it the day you call him, he won't have one ounce more the day he resigns." Personal experience has confirmed his wisdom.

While one who has no judgment cannot learn it, one who has some judgment can cultivate it. In order to cultivate judgment, however, a person must focus not on judgment itself, but rather on its component qualities. Of these there are several.

First, good judgment involves an intelligent assessment of both issues and risks. A minister must deal with issues. Just as every minister is a theologian, every minister is also an ethicist. He must understand both the great social issues of the day and the timeless personal issues of the flock. He must have a solid grasp of the Bible, particularly Jesus' great ethical principle of love. He must also develop a keen insight into the devastating effects of sin, both social and personal. He must be attentive to the details of various issues so that he can make informed judgments and not knee-jerk, crowd-following reactions. He must react to issues emotionally, of course, but only after he understands them mentally. He must also understand enough about ethics to make sound judgments about the relative importance of various issues. Since all issues cannot be addressed at once, the minister must be able to choose issues prudently.

Second, good judgment involves sensitivity. The minister must have keen antennae in at least three areas: 1) He must be alert to the devastating effects of evil in the lives of his people. He must be enraged by dishonesty and artificiality. He must see the cancer of greed for what it is. He must feel the desperation of the alcoholic and his or her family. He must weep over his people's bigotry and hardheartedness. He must sense the guilt and estrangement caused by sexual immorality. Without this, his ministry will be ethically irrelevant. 2) He must be alert to the levels of resistance he is likely to encounter if he takes a prophetic stand. Unfortunately, many ministers use their fear of resistance as an excuse for never taking a stand, while others charge in where angels fear to tread and, therefore, sacrifice their ministries over petty issues. Ideally, a minister should be keenly aware of the cost of prophecy, intelligently calculate the risks of a prophetic stand, and then speak boldly only when the Holy Spirit dictates. 3) He must be alert to the spirit of God. The Christian ministry does not call others to a higher *human* standard of behavior, it calls others to *God's* standard of behavior. The minister who is insensitive to the Holy Spirit will never understand this. He will listen to human voices rather than the voice of God. His ethical standards will be those of popular culture rather than those of God.

A third quality which is a component of good judgment is realism. Idealism is essential and should never be dismissed lightly. An idealistic vision provides the ethical push which drives us to work for the realization of Jesus' prayer, "Thy kingdom come, . . . On earth as it is in heaven" (Matt. 6:10).

Nevertheless, good judgment requires a healthy dose of realism. Where are people's attitudes about race, pornography, integrity, sexuality, and family life? Where would we like to lead people and how can we get them there? These are the questions of the realist. Anger says, "I don't care what they think. I'm going to take my stand." Fear says, "If I just preach salvation, morality will take care of itself." Realism says, "Let's start where the people are and see how we can move them to where God wants them to be."

A final component of judgment is fear. No officer in combat can make an effective judgment about whether to mount an attack or how to mount it without a healthy fear of the dangers that await. Neither can any minister decide when to mount an attack on evil or how to mount it unless he is afraid of the consequences. Fear, however, must be controlled. Uncontrolled fear results in retreating soldiers on the battlefield and retreating prophets in the church; but controlled fear contributes to an intelligent assessment of risks and solid judgments about when to take them.

Judgment has many components, but no analysis of its parts is an adequate explanation of the whole. It is a gift from God which must be guarded, nurtured, and used. Without it God's Word cannot be proclaimed.

3. *Prophetic ministry has a high cost.*—This is especially true of a pulpit ministry. Over the years I have read a number of books and articles about confronting ethical issues in the pulpit. The problem with many of these articles, however, is that they are designed to explain how to preach prophetically while incurring no cost. This simply is not possible to do if one wishes to change anything in the world.

For instance, it is possible to avoid criticism by preaching only on issues about which the congregation agrees with the minister. But what is gained by this kind of preaching? At best it is not prophetic, and at worst it is no more than the feeding of the congregation's prejudice. And yet this has perhaps been the most common sin of many pulpits. It is also possible for a minister to minimize the cost of prophecy by veiling prophetic utterances in such soft language that they are not understood. I tried this approach once and failed miserably. During the civil rights struggle of the 1960s, I preached in a small rural church one Sunday and slipped in an off-handed remark to the effect that whatever one might think about the race issue, surely all could agree that God wanted us to love one another in spite of differences in the color of our skin. Some time later one of the members reacted to the sermon: "The only sermon I ever heard you preach which I disagreed with was when you preached that sermon where you said we should love niggers." He had understood the sermon well, and he indicted my softpedaling of the gospel more than he ever knew.

As little as we may like it, it does cost something to address the great issues of any day. By its very nature confrontation offends the perpetrators of evil and arouses their hostile response. This is true when the minister must challenge unethical attitudes and behavior within the church, and it is also true when he must lead the church to challenge unethical attitudes and behavior in society.

Confronting ethical issues may be costly, but it is not an optional part of the ministry. It goes with the territory. Those who follow the One who called Herod a fox, who applied the label *hypocrite* unapologetically, and who ran the money changers out of the Temple, should not expect a ministry free of confrontation. And those who follow the One who was nailed to the cross of Calvary, should not expect a ministry free from persecution or rejection.

4. *Success in confronting moral issues should be measured in terms of effectiveness.*—There are those who honestly feel that success should be measured only in terms of faithfulness to the gospel. Others believe that success should be measured in terms of the professional survival of the minister, and still others feel that the only sure sign of success is martyrdom.

None of these are adequate measurements. Faithfulness is important, of course, and sometimes it is all we can do. If we cannot obliterate racism or rid a city of a corrupt administration, we can at least be faithful in our stand for righteousness, and we certainly have the right to feel good about that faithfulness. But it is a lie to claim that we have succeeded in our confrontation with evil. We can best cope with our failure not by redefining it as success, but by admitting it to be failure, and by placing our faith in the One who alone is able to conquer evil.

The call to ministry is a call to make a difference. Ministers are responsible not merely to fight evil, but to defeat it where possible. A large part of the impotence of the modern church is due to the fact that we no longer believe we are responsible to win the war for the right. If Christians who lived in America in the days before the Civil War had been content to speak against evil faithfully without defeating it, we would still have slavery in this country and we would have to be hypocrites to sing of "the land of the free and the home of the brave." If Martin Luther King, Jr., had been content to hold up his standard of righteousness faithfully without actually defeating evil, the state of racial justice in this land might be a full generation behind where it is today. If Moses had been concerned only to speak about justice without establishing it for the Hebrews he would not have said to Pharaoh, "Let my people go," but something like, "Treat my people nice." God is concerned about more than just a witness to justice; He is concerned to establish it. This is the message that thundered from the Red Sea as the waters closed over Pharaoh's soldiers. This is the message that rode into Israel with Babylon's armies and rose from the prophet's tongues like a flaming fire.

The mark of success of a church confronting homelessness is people with homes. The mark of success of a church which concerned for the hungry is people with full stomachs. The mark of success of a church which cares about the family is stable homes. The mark of success of a church which is combating pornography is clean newsstands. The mark of success of a church which hates racism is an usher of one skin color sincerely welcoming a family of another to worship. Effectiveness, not merely faithfulness, is the mark of success.

5. *Many tools for confrontation are at the minister's disposal.*—

While many ministers dismiss their own profession as uninfluential, they have a number of powerful tools available to them. The pulpit is one such tool but it is not the only one. The minister also confronts ethical issues through such avenues of ministry as counseling, administration, public involvement, and personal relationships.

The pulpit is a special place of influence. Not only does the minister have the influence of any good orator, but he also has an audience which returns to hear him speak week after week. This may increase the difficulty of preaching, but it also increases the potential for influence. I once heard of a congressman who said that if he had even fifty people who would listen to him for half an hour a week, he could change public opinion in his district. Most ministers have just such an opportunity.

In addition to the natural influence every podium has, the pulpit carries special influence as the podium where God's Word is spoken. I remember staying after church one Sunday as a child and approaching the pulpit for the first time. My parents were not sure I should be there at all, but they insisted that if I was to be near the pulpit I should behave with a reverence which at least matched that required in worship. This kind of attitude reflects more than magic and superstition, it reflects a deeply-rooted respect for the pulpit as one avenue through which the Word of God enters the world. When the preacher stands to preach, he does not stand to speak for himself; he stands to speak for God. To the extent that he does this faithfully, his words are empowered beyond his own human limitations. How else can one explain the effectiveness of sermons which confront the deep-seated prejudices of the hearers? From any human standard of judgment, these sermons should fail. They succeed because they are blessed of God. Whenever the minister addresses ethical issues from the pulpit, the power of God Himself is at the preacher's disposal.

The minister can also help people to apply the faith to life in the counseling room. While any good counselor must refrain from the temptation to make decisions for those seeking help, one of the distinctives of the pastoral counselor is that he is called on to serve as an ethical guide. Contrary to the opinions of some, ethical guidance is not inappropriate in the counseling room. Christian ethics is Christian precisely because it is *for* people. It is inappropriate, even sinful, to impose one's own commitments on another in a judgmental and manipulative spirit, but to sit with one whose life has been crippled by the arthritic power of evil and to fail to point the way to righteousness is also a sin.

The administrative load of the average minister has increased immeasurably in the last generation with the proliferation of church staffs and programs. Administration may seem at first glance to remove the minister from ethical involvement, but it is precisely in the administrative arena that many ethical issues are encountered. Here the minister has a unique opportunity to organize people to do good. Here the minister confronts a variety of practical ethical problems: How does one supervise staff in a manner which places value both on the person and on the task? How does one deal with a moral problem in the life of a staff member? What are the ethics of pay for church employees? How can a committee dispute be settled in a manner befitting the body of Christ? The minister as administrator does not stop being the minister as ethicist. In fact, in the administrative arena the minister is required to go beyond the level of theorizing and advice giving; in the administrative arena he is required actually to make tough ethical decisions.

Another tool for ethical influence is available to the minister through his public ministry. Nearly every minister is asked to pray at a host of public events, to participate in public ceremonies, to make comments to the press on various moral issues, and to be generally visible in the community. All of these opportunities provide avenues for an ethical witness. As one who is seen by much of the public as a kind of moral authority figure, the minister can use these events either to provide legitimation for community moral standards or to challenge them. This is no mean opportunity.

Of course, personal relationships thrust every person into confrontations with ethical issues, but the minister's personal confrontations with these issues are often matters of public concern. This makes many a minister feel that the world has made him the victim of a double standard: What is acceptable behavior for others is not acceptable for him. In the eyes of God, of course, we are all judged against the same standard, but realism demands that we recognize that there are and always will be special moral expectations of the minister. The minister who sins is perceived to be guilty of more than the sin itself: he is also perceived to be guilty of a profound lack of integrity since he has chosen a role which symbolizes righteousness for the community while also choosing to behave immorally. The minister may or may not see this as fair, but it is the way things are.

In the providence of God, His ministers have been given more opportunities for influence than come to most people. In recent years, there has been much complaining from the clergy about their declining influence. In my opinion, however, the greater problem has been our declining courage to use the influence which is at our disposal. In a world dominated by consumer-oriented religion it is easy to let courage decline, but a God-oriented faith demands that the minister diligently use all the tools of influence he has been given.

6. *The minister must possess integrity in order to confront ethical issues effectively.*—Effectiveness aside, a minister must have integrity in order to confront ethical issues at all! Most would rather leave them alone. We know instinctively that there is a cost to prophetic ministry, and while we may admire others who are willing to pay that cost, we are not particularly eager to pay it ourselves. Only a robust integrity can propel a minister into the sticky, life-threatening, person-destroying issues of the day.

It is also true, however, that integrity is necessary for *effectiveness* in the task of applying the gospel. If people feel that the minister's ethical pronouncements are self-serving or insincere, his effectiveness is in jeopardy. If, on the other hand, he is perceived to be speaking from a deep sense of integrity, he is far more likely to gain a hearing for an unpopular idea.

Integrity, of course, is more than honesty, never less. It is that sense of wholeness which allows a person to be at peace. It is the basic source of that much-coveted virtue of self-esteem. Integrity is harmony, in this particular case the harmony of words with deeds, the harmony of words and deeds with the soul, and the harmony of the soul with God. Without this harmony ethical confrontation is a cacophony which drives away the audience, or tinkling cymbal which amounts to nothing. With this harmony of integrity, prophetic ministry is a symphony, perhaps of stern mood and serious tone, but nonetheless a symphony of exceptional beauty and incredible truth.

These six observations are nothing more than a few preliminary thoughts. Approaches and applications may vary, but this much is certain: Christian ministry which avoids ethical encounter is neither Christian nor ministry. After all, we are followers of the One who announced His own ministry with these words:

> The Spirit of the Lord is upon me,
> because he has anointed me to
> preach good news to the poor.
> He has sent me to proclaim release to the captives
> and recovering of sight to the blind,
> to set at liberty those who are oppressed,
> to proclaim the acceptable year of the Lord (Luke 4:18-19).

When courage fails and strength wanes, when confrontations with evil appear ominous and threatening, the Lord who spoke these words leads us on. The One who confronted all the powers of darkness on a cross will give adequate strength to all His servants who are willing to follow Him in confronting the grave moral issues of today's world.

Notes

1. The masculine pronoun is used in this chapter to avoid awkwardness of expression.
2. Thomas Merton, *Contemplative Prayer* (Garden City, New York: Doubleday & Co., 1971), 39.

10

Women as Agents of Change

by C. Anne Davis

Introduction

With the celebration of the end of World War II in May 1945, peace and prosperity gave birth to a surge in the amount and rate of change in America. In the last half of this century, this surge came of age. No person or institution escaped its repercussions. Its ever-present intensity left in its wake a society groping for stability and searching for the familiar.

As a result, Americans have a love/hate relationship with change. Few people are willing to give up the gains garnered during this period of rapid change. However, during the last fifteen years, the majority of Americans have elected leaders who promise to check the rate of change and reinstate the past.

As is often true of societies, this reaction to change has become reactionary. In an effort to compensate for too much change, the populace has called for too much return to the past. In embracing this myopic valuing of the past, the American people have fallen into the same trap present in runaway change—taking off in a direction without being guided by a careful questioning of what is truth, what is best, and what is enduringly moral.

Thesis

A discussion of women as agents of change within this volatile milieu is difficult. It seems safe to say that there is no one view on the subject which enjoys majority support. Therefore, the thesis of this chapter can only be viewed as one opinion among many. At best, it may serve to stimulate others to think more carefully about women as agents of change.

The thesis is 1) that women primarily function as change agents in informal ways at microlevels; 2) that this informal role at the microlevel results from and contributes to stereotypic cultural norms about the acceptable role of women; 3) that written history does not provide a record of the role of women as change agents; 4) that women have not made a significant contribution to change-agent theory because they have in some cases been shut out of the process and in some cases been too quick to accommodate societal norms; 5) that women have a responsibility to contribute female perspectives to a reshaping of change-agent theory; and 6) that women will choose to address such a reshaping only when they come to appreciate the healthy gifts of their cultural heritage while defusing, through understanding, its dysfunctional powers of constraint.

A number of questions need to be addressed in support of this thesis. What is a change agent? What is known about women as agents of change? What is the body of literature related to women as agents of change? What contributions have women made to change theory? What is suspiciously masculine in current change-agent theory? What can women contribute that is different? What are some of the dysfunctional powers which tend to constrain a reshaping of change theory?

The Change Agent

As early as 1947, this term was coined by social scientists working at the National Training Laboratories of the National Education Association. They referred to helping professionals who intentionally intervened in change processes as "change agents."[1]

Since then, the use of the term has been broadened to include anyone who consciously intervenes in a situation with the intention of guiding the change processes in some predetermined direction. Qualifiers such as the agent of *social* change or the agent of *organizational* change evidence this expanding definition. For example, Hessel writes about the Christian as an agent of social change, the "person called to be a social reformer . . . who is concerned about the large issues of our time without losing sight of the children, the poor, the sick, and the old who ask for personal care and attention."[2] Lippitt, Bennis, Benne, Chin, Kettner, Daley, and Nichols are leaders in the literature related to organizational change.[3]

Regardless of the definition, the term change agent has consistently been used to denote a role function rather than a title or position. Dickson states that when the change agent function is "formalized into a position within an organization the term change agent is dropped in favor of a position designation."[4]

The History of Women as Agents of Change

A search of the literature revealed no comprehensive, scholarly record of the history of women as agents of change. It seems that the history of the contribution of women as agents of change suffers from the same dilemma as Afro-American history. Women and Afro-Americans have been on the back side of the American agenda. The mainstream has been Anglo-American and patriarchal; therefore, its history has been traced through the activities, decisions, and accomplishments of white males. Of course there are a few exceptions to this and some women and Afro-Americans were noted in the history books. All school children know of Betsy Ross's legendary sewing skills, Pocahontas' bravery, and Booker T. Washington's genius with the peanut. However, these pale in comparison to the coverage given to President Washington's leadership, Captain John Smith's explorations, and Teddy Roosevelt's exploits.

While efforts have been made during the last two decades to reconstruct the history of the contributions of women in American society, materials related to the finer points, the sharper pictures, accounts of the everyday life of American women as agents of change are lost forever. Reconstructed history is, at best, much like trying to envision a sky from a few stars and several sunrises.

For example, most of the written history related to the role of Southern Baptist women as agents of change is found in their obituaries and in archival materials of Woman's Missionary Union. History of the contributions of women in general is subsumed in the history of the various peaks within the feminist movement occurring after the 1750s.

A study of the obituaries of women found in state Baptist papers outline accomplishments of ordinary women in Southern Baptist life. Comparable accounts are not found in the classics of Southern Baptist history. Leon McBeth, a respected historian of Southern Baptists wrote a book entitled, *Women in Baptist Life.*[5] In this book he attempted to inject historical material on women into the mainstream of Southern Baptist history and in so doing recognized its previous absence.

Catherine Allen, in her book, *A Century to Celebrate,* calls attention to the historical material in the archives of Woman's Missionary Union.

> Why has Woman's Missionary Union been ignored in the footnotes of historical writing? The answer can be found in the fact that men have been the primary writers of history. Even the experts have not yet learned their way into the archives of WMU, where an enormous body of published literature and unbroken minutes lie unmined.[6]

Often the historical accounts of the peak periods in the feminist movement are written from a devaluing position. A good example of this is the devaluing of the role of Jane Addams in the development of the discipline of sociology at the University of Chicago at the turn of the century. Reconstructed history indicates that Addams carried out the first systematic demographic studies and social investigations of Chicago neighborhoods. These findings were foundational in the development of sociology at the University of Chicago. However, early in the effort to build the theory, Addams was shut out of the process and forced to take refuge with the "other women" carrying out the work of Hull House. Mary Jo Deegan provides supportive evidence for this reconstructed history in *Jane Addams and the Men of the Chicago School, 1892-1918.*[7]

Women's Contributions to Change-Agent Theory

The current theories of change agentry lack the perspectives of women. A review of the literature revealed only one book written by a woman which specifically addressed change and the role of the change agent—Elaine Dickson's book entitled, *Say No, Say Yes to Change* published by Broadman Press in 1982. Dickson's book is a popularized version of her Ed.D. dissertation, "An Analysis of the Change Agent Function in Church Organizations." An analysis of the 492 entries in her forty-one-page bibliography yielded additional support to the thesis that current change theory lacks the perspectives of women. The 492 entries included only nineteen female writers. Of these nineteen, eight were listed as second authors among several authors.[8]

Searches of Women in History, American History and Life, Sociological Abstracts, and Social Work Abstracts using women, change agents, and the United States as search indicators produced no entries. Additional searches of these computerized data bases using the indicators of women and social movements produced fifty-three entries. These entries are focused primarily on the temperance movement, the peace movement, the feminist movement, and women's rights. A number of these entries related to women who lived or are living in countries other than the United States.

This review of the literature seems to indicate that if a body of materials exists related to women's contributions to change theory that this literature is somehow submerged in writings that do not call specific attention to women as agents of change. For example, women have historically found a role as agents of change in and through the professions of social work, nursing, teaching, and other helping professions.[9] Individuals in these professions exercise authority, leadership, influence, and power through the role of change agent. Why have these contributions remained submerged in the scholarly literature?

Perhaps it is for the same reason that the public's perception of these professions has not changed. All of these groups have spent considerable energy and resources during the last two decades in generally unsuccessful attempts to expand their public images to include being seen as leaders, as influential, as powerful, and as essential to a higher quality of life for all Americans. It must be that powerful cultural constraints about gender differences are at work.[10]

Selected Perspectives of Women
Positive Contributions to the Reshaping of
the Function of the Change Agent

Roslyn Chernesky studied 381 women administrators in top-level positions in human services agencies in New York. In 1986 she presented her findings to the National Conference on Women's Issues sponsored by the National Association of Social Work meeting in Atlanta as follows:

1. Women do in fact believe that they bring to their administrative positions special qualities, values, or perspectives because they are women.
2. They believe that they act on their own uniqueness, doing things and carrying out their administrative tasks differently than their male counterparts.
3. The study provided strong support for the notion that women administrators bring to their positions women's experience of caring.
4. Women anticipate, interpret, and respond to the needs of others which encourages and requires a sensitivity and empathy toward others, and a nurturing and cooperative attitude.
5. Women see themselves on a continuum rather than as opposed to others.[11]

These findings give support to the choice of three female perspectives as illustrative of the contributions women might make to the reshaping of change theory and the role of the change agent. These are 1) the high value women in general place on cooperation and building and maintaining relationships, 2) the tendency for women to make decisions based on personally held values, and 3) the freedom women have in communicating their affective side as well as their cognitive side.

1. The high value women place on building and maintaining relationships is evidenced in Georgia Sassen's critique of Horner's popular research on "success anxiety" in women. In 1964 Matina Horner, an experimental psychologist at the University of Michigan, was working on the relationship between motivation and achievement. She and other researchers at Michigan were puzzled by the results of their research on women subjects. No two sets of women came up with similar results on the test models designed by the researchers.[12] This inconsistency in findings was not present among the male subjects tested. The researchers concluded from the high-anxiety scores turned in by female subjects that women have a "hopeless will to fail."[13]

Horner was not satisfied with this interpretation and in later research with the Thematic Apperception Tests found that women experience a high level of anxiety over success. From these findings she concluded that the confounding variable in the earlier Michigan study was not a "will to fail" but rather "a fear of success" in situations involving competition with men which might result in social rejection or loss of femininity.[14] Sassen offers the following description of what happened next.

> Horner's data were widely accepted as proof that women feared or were anxious over the expectation of success. Her idea was popularized in the late sixties by articles in *Time, Newsweek,* the *New York Times Magazine, Ms.,* and even the *National Enquirer.* Fear of success became a common independent variable in experiments reported at professional meetings. . . . Fear of success was accepted as a variable that could be quantified, and a large body of scholarly literature developed on the subject even in the midst of debate as to what it was, in what form it existed, and how it would be measured.[15]

Sassen questioned Horner's identification of the cause of the anxiety. Rather than seeing the anxiety as caused by a fear of success, Sassen saw this anxiety as a result of a fear of competitive success gained at high emotional cost. She thought that women were not simply afraid but rather "unable to take competitive success and construct around it a vision, a new way of making sense, to which they could feel personally committed." In other words, women are more oriented toward "preserving and fostering relationships than winning."[16]

Carol Gilligan in her book entitled, *In a Different Voice: Psychological Theory and Woman's Development,* says it this way:

> . . . male and female voices typically speak of the importance of different truths, the former of the role of separation as it defines and empowers the self, the latter of the ongoing process of attachment that creates and sustains the human community.[17]

Chernesky posits that "part of the female identity is to recognize ongoing responsibility for others, to protect others from being hurt and exploited, and to maintain a web of relationships without excluding anyone."[18] Jane Farley presents another perspective on this relationship variable. She says:

> . . . if you ask a group of women what is a team, they will usually say it means: "Everybody should cooperate to get the job done," "Everybody pitches in, doing whatever they can to help others." . . . But if you ask a ten year old boy what a team is, he will often answer in baseball terminology. "There's a pitcher, a catcher, a first baseman." . . . He already knows that a team is a very rigid structure and has a prescribed function, and that each player covers his own position and nobody else's. He does not talk about everybody pitching in to get the job done.[19]

In the reshaping of change theory and the function of change agent, the female perspective would give more attention to relationships and community building. Women's perspectives would make the change process more inclusive and establish community building as a part of change theory. This would mean that the inclusion of minorities, marginal groups, ethnic groups, and oppressed people would be essential to change efforts. The empowerment of these participants would require a concept of shared power rather than a powerful elite group of key leaders.

Change theory reshaped by women could be expected to be directed by a sensitivity and sympathy for the needs of others. This sensitivity would involve more networking with more people with a careful monitoring of the process. Women could be expected to focus attention on the process and trust the outcomes if the process is followed. It is extremely difficult to protect the people involved and honor their needs through the process if it is being violated by unilateral actions of individuals no matter how noble their intentions.

2. The tendency among females to make decisions based on personally held values is the second perspective to be reviewed. One of the factors in the highly regarded and much used Myers-Briggs Type Indicator inventories the way people make decisions.[20] This decision-making style is measured on a continuum of thinking-feeling. Those individuals on the thinking end of the continuum "tend to become logical, objective and consistent, and to make . . . decisions by analyzing and weighing the facts, including the unpleasant ones."[21] Those persons on the feeling end of the continuum "tend to become sympathetic, appreciative, and tactful and to give great weight . . . to personally held values . . . including those of other persons."[22]

The thinking-feeling continuum is the only factor of the four inventoried in the Myers-Briggs that requires a different scoring template for men and women. This is not surprising since the American cultural norms ascribe logical decision making to the category of characteristics of males and any nonlogical based decision-making style to the categories of female characteristics. While the Myers-Briggs Type Indicator is quick to establish that neither end of this continuum is better than the other, society does not.

Sometimes decisions need to be made based on a logical, objective analysis of the facts. Sometimes decisions need to be made based on a sympathetic appreciation of personally held values. For example, if the roof leaks, a logical objective analysis of the facts will indicate that the appropriate action is to repair the roof before further damage is done to the building, its contents, and its utility. On the other hand, some decisions need to be made based on what is held to be right and just even if it is is illogical. For example it is hard to build a logical, objective economic analysis which supports giving your possessions away to feed and clothe the poor.

In terms of the functioning of the change agent, these data could have negative as well as positive outcomes. If all decisions are made based on the "feeling" type, the function of the change agent would suffer from a lack of appropriate objectivity and analysis. If all decisions are made based on the "thinking" type, the function of the change agent would suffer from a lack of needed reflection on what is right and just. The positive point being made here is that the female perspective would bring a needed corrective to many change efforts—this corrective being that logical, objective analysis is not the only basis on which to make sound decisions concerning change efforts.

3. The breadth of emotional expression is the last of the three contributions to be discussed. In 1970 Layne Longfellow, Anthony Rose, and Terry Van Orshoven developed a simulation game called, *Body Talk*.[23] This game gives participants an opportunity to test out their ability to communicate feelings through body actions such as facial expressions, movements, and gestures. The developers of the game used indifference, fear, hate, hope, admiration, contentment, loneliness, joy, anger, shyness, sorrow, frustration, and love to comprise the list of feelings. After using this game in a coed class, Davis asked the class to group the list of feelings into three subgroups according to American cultural norms as to those most acceptable for public express by males, by females, and those acceptable to both groups.[24]

While this exercise cannot be considered as valid research, it did raise an interesting issue about the possible differences in the width of culturally acceptable female and male emotional ranges. For the most part, both men and women labeled indifference, anger, and frustration as acceptable feelings for men to express in public; shyness, joy, loneliness, fear, hate, contentment, hope, and love as acceptable feelings for women to express in public; and sorrow and admiration as acceptable for both groups.

Subsequent testing of these findings through observations of people would indicate that it is safe to assume that American cultural norms accept from women a wider band of emotional expression than they do from men. In the last fifteen years there has been a widening of this band for males; however, it is still much narrower than that of women.

For this wider band, women pay a not-so-subtle price—they are considered less stable emotionally than men and less predictable. What really happens here is that women are not less stable but they are less predictable. For example, if one is interacting with a male in a situation where feelings will be expressed, the man can be expected to respond with one of about five feelings—indifference, anger, frustration, admiration, or sorrow. Women, on the other hand, may respond in similar situations out of a pool of about ten emotions ranging from love to hate, joy to sorrow, and so forth. Since a woman has many more ways of responding with feeling, it stands to reason that one would be less able to predict which of these possible feelings she will choose to express. This does not indicate that women are emotionally unstable! It does indicate that they are different!

Many women working in primarily male work settings have had to narrow this band of possible emotional expression in order to provide the level of predictability men supervisors need to have in order to perceive women as being stable and mature individuals. What women have to be careful of is making this band of expressed feelings so narrow that they are viewed as "acting like a man." To do this would compromise their sense of self as female and negate the gift of community building which they have that requires the expression of all human feelings.

In terms of change theory and the reshaping of the function of the change agent women can be expected to contribute significant skills as communicators. The inclusion of affective material will make for a more open pattern of communication. Negative feelings that often cause people to revert to old patterns rather than internalize the change will more likely be dealt with in the change process. Words and feelings will receive more attention.

Key Mitigating Issues

Cultural Patterns of Socialization

The socialization process is the method by which a society teaches its young the values, knowledge, skills, and norms needed to survive and contribute to the culture of that society. It is how people learn to be people. This process of socialization, while essential to the continuity, stability, growth, and change within the total society, is often the carrier of dysfunctional patterns for the socialization of subsystems within the society.

The socialization patterns in the colonial South are used to illustrate how such a dysfunctional socialization pattern operates to curb the change-agent function among white females. Certainly the South has changed since colonial days. However, there are trailing influences which will strongly influence white women born and reared in the South. These influences work against efforts of these women to intentionally engage in macrolevel overt change strategies.

The work of Queen and Habenstein in their book entitled, *The Family in Various Cultures,* describe the differences in family patterns developed in two regions of colonial America—New England and the South.[25] A summary comparison of these two models of settlement are presented to illustrate how each is unique and to set the stage for an in-depth discussion of the model followed in the South. This extensive review of the Southern model will outline issues these women need to understand and intentionally address in shaping their roles as agents of change.

The New England region was settled primarily by Puritans in family groups who developed a village style of living. The New England Town Meeting was the structure through which community decisions were made. Individuals were regarded as members of a family group.

Households had "very inclusive functions—educational, religious, protective, regulatory, procreational—but with heavy emphasis on economics." While women were generally responsible for the home, there are records of women establishing businesses outside the home.[26]

The settlement pattern followed in the South was quite different. The colonial South was settled by adventuring white males seeking their fortunes. These men were known as cavaliers. The society developed as a layered one with first families, yeomen, a fringe of poor whites, indentured servants, and black slaves holding position of descending status. Plantations, rather than villages, were the social structure.[27]

As these cavaliers began their plantations as single men seeking their fortunes, the primary population was made up of single white male owners, male and female slaves, male and female Native Americans, and the poor white male and female fringe often grouped with the slave population.

As these groups settled more and more of the land, a society developed around the plantation model. As the layers of the society were put in place, it became evident that one group was obvious by its absence—white females wives for the owners.

The owners of the plantations began to look for women to be the first ladies of the plantations to complete the quasi-caste system. It would be the task of these women to establish the aristocracy of the South. To do this, these women would need to have experience in living the aristocratic life. The only available place to get such properly trained women was Europe.

Arrangements were made for shiploads of women to be brought from Europe to become the "Southern Belles." These women were to instill in the South the European aristocratic way of life. In addition, they were to bear legitimate heirs who would inherit the plantation, preserve the Southern way of life, and keep the family name alive. They were to bring social graces and charm to a crude and hard New World and to husbands who were "rough around the edges."

The dilemma was what to do with the informal societal structure which had grown up before these women were imported. The solution adopted in the South was simply to let the two sets of structures coexist.

These coexisting societal pattern provided plots for numerous novels on the antebellum period. *Gone with the Wind, Beulah Land,* and *Roots* are some examples. This literature tells of white owners who carried on dual lives living publicly with the "Southern Belles" to whom they were lawfully married and living privately with women of the slave quarters. Queen and Habenstein state that the cavaliers continued to live by the sexual mores of the period which allowed infidelity in marriage.[28]

Some means had to be found to deal with such incongruity in the societal structures and values if the society was to remain stable. The thing that would hold all this together was the community's willingness to establish and live with strong boundaries between what was public life—the aristocracy—and what was private life—the society in place before the white women were imported. Everyone knew about it but no one talked about it and, as long as it was not talked about it was not reality.

Two very different role models for women coexisted in the South during this period. One role model was the public wife—a woman was to be a beautiful, charming, very feminine wife who ensured that etiquette was followed, who gave public deference to her husband, who demonstrated a certain degree of helplessness and dependence, and who bore legitimate heirs. The other role model was cast along the lines of the private wife called for a woman who was a real partner in sex and companionship—a wife to whom a husband could go to share his hurts and disappointments and anything which would be seen in the public society as weakness, such as the need for nurture. She was to be a strong woman, a survivor in the face of helplessness, a woman who asked little for herself or her children, and one who could deal with the hard realities of a hard life.

Affective norms remain alive in societies long after the cognitive awareness of the practices which created them have vanished. This was the case in the South. Certainly these norms have been somewhat mortified but there are still trailing influences.

A white woman growing up in the South still has instilled in her a strong sense of what is "public" and what is "private." She knows that some things are not talked about at all. She knows that if something is not verbalized that it is not as real as something that can be discussed in public. She can live with something wrong better if it is not brought out into the open through speech.

This socialization pattern has several significant factors related to the role of these women as agents of change.

White women born and reared in the South still have two very different role models from which to choose. This often results in role ambiguity among Southern white women. They can either be the prototype of the Southern Belle or the prototype of the private wife. It is difficult, if not impossible, to be both at one time.

While changes have come, the society still gives these the strong message that in public she is to be the mother, the hostess, the charming, somewhat dependent female, the keeper of the roles of etiquette, the person who bring honor and pride to her husband and family, and the person who makes up for the rough edges of her husband. If she will accept this role, she will be loved, supplied with emotional support, given abundant recognition, accepted, and protected.

She can be the real companion, strong leader, and change agent as long as she does in the privacy of her home. If she seeks to be exercise authority, to be a strong leader, and or to be economically independent in public she will experience subtle, and sometimes not so subtle, efforts from others to put her back in her place.

The point to be made here is that the characteristics which the role of change agent conjures up are more nearly parallel to the model of the private wife than they are to the public wife. Women reared from birth in the South tend to lean more toward the model of the public wife. White women reared in the South, unless they consciously choose otherwise, will probably fashion a role of change agent which is more private than public. In other words, they will try to bring about change from the private sectors of action rather than the public. Those who choose to be public and out front in their change efforts will incur the wrath of those men and women living in the community who still hold to the taboos and mores of days past which say that "nice women" do not do such things and that if she does, she is trying to act "like a man."

If women can understand the kind of cultural constraints outlined here, there is hope that they can lessen the influence of these constraints and choose to be public in their change-agent strategies in structures and systems which call for prophetic actions.

Summary

A discussion of women as agents of change is the volatile climate of America's love/hate relationship with change is difficult. No one view can garner majority support. The ideas presented in this chapter are first words, not last words. At best they may stimulate others to think more carefully about women as agents of change and contributors to change theory. Not to do this careful thinking may well add to America's continuing to follow the pattern of taking off in a direction which is not guided by a careful questioning of what is truth, what is best, what is enduringly moral and Christian.

Notes

1. B. Elaine Dickson, "An Analysis of the Change Agent Function in Church Organization." (Ed.D. diss., The Southern Baptist Theological Seminary, 1972), 180.
2. Dieter T. Hessel, *Social Ministry* (Philadelphia: The Westminster Press, 1973), 26.
3. See Gordon L. Lippitt, *Organizational Renewal: Achieving Viability in a Changing World* (New York: Appleton-Century-Crofts, 1969); Gordon L. Lippitt, *Visualizing Change: Model Building and the Change Process* (Fairfax, Va.: National Training Laboratories Learning Resources Corporation, 1973); Warren G. Bennis, *Changing Organizations*, (New York: McGraw-Hill, 1966); and Warren G. Bennis, Kenneth D. Benne, and Robert Chin, *The Planning of Change* (New York: Holt, Rinehart, and Winston, 1969); and Peter Kettner, John M. Daley, and Ann Weaver Nichols, *Initiating Change in Organizations and Communities* (Monterey, Ca.: Brooks/Cole Publishing Company,

1985).

4. Dickson, 183.

5. Leon McBeth, *Women in Baptist Life* (Nashville: Broadman Press, 1979).

6. Catherine Allen, *A Century to Celebrate: History of Woman's Missionary Union* (Birmingham, Al.: Woman's Missionary Union, SBC, 1987), i.

7. Mary Jo Deegan, *Jane Addams and the Men of the Chicago School, 1892-1918* (N. J.: Transaction, Inc., 1988).

8. Dickson, 279-319.

9. Two other volumes on change were located, both written by women for micro-level change interventions, which demonstrate this point. The first is *The Change Process* by Peggy Papp, a social worker with the Ackerman Institute for Family Therapy, published in 1983 by Guilford Press. The other example is a book by psychotherapist Ellen Y. Siegelman written while she was in private practice in San Francisco. Siegelman's book was published in 1983 by Harper & Row.

10. For an in-depth discussion of the universality of women being considered secondary to men, see Liesa Stamm and Carol D. Ryff, eds., *Social Power and Influence of Women* (Boulder, Co.: Westview Press, 1984).

11. Roslyn H. Chernesky, "Women's Influence on the Administration of Human Services," Unpublished paper presented to the 1986 National Association of Social Workers's Conference on Women's Issues, Atlanta, Ga., 14.

12. Vivian Gornick, "Why Women Fear Success," *New York Magazine,* December 20, 1971.

13. Ibid.

14. Georgia Sassen, "Success Anxiety in Women: A Constructivist Interpretation of its Source and its Significance," *Harvard Educational Review* 50 (February 1980): 13-24.

15. Sassen, 14; Roslyn H. Chernesky, "Women Administrators in Social Work," in *Tactics and Techniques of Community Practice*, Fred M. Cox, John L Erlich, Jack Rothman, and John E. Tropman, eds. (Itasca, Ill.: F. E. Peacock Publishers, Inc., 1984), 435-37.

16. Sassen, 18.

17. Carol Gilligan, *In a Different Voice: Psychological Theory and Woman's Development* (Cambridge: Harvard University Press, 1982), 156.

18. Chernesky, 4.

19. Betty Lehan Harragan, "Women and Men at Work: Jockeying for Position," *The Woman in Management*, Jane Farley, ed. (New York: ILR Press, 1983), 18.

20. Kathryn Briggs and Isabell Briggs Myers. *Myers-Briggs Type Indicator* (Palo Alto, Ca.: Consulting Psychologist Press, 1976).

21. I. Briggs, *Introduction to Type* (Gainesville, Fl.: Center for Applications of Psychological Type, 1976), 4.

22. I. Briggs, 2.

23. Layne A. Longfellow, Anthony Rose, and Terry Van Orshoven. *Body Talk* (Del Mar, Ca.: Communications/Research/Machines/Inc., 1970).

24. Anne Davis used this exercise with classes of males and females enrolled in the social-work major in the then School of Religious Education at The Southern Baptist Theological Seminary, Louisville, Kentucky in the Spring semester of 1975. Approximately twenty-five students participated. Approximately half of the class was female and half the class was male.

25. Stuart A. Queen and Robert W. Habenstein, *The Family in Various Cultures* (New York: J. B. Lippincott Company, 1974), 294-329.

26. Queen and Habenstein, 295-314.

27. Ibid., 314-26.

28. Ibid.

||| 11 |||

Ministering with Public-School Adolescents

by G. Wade Rowlett

Adolescents not only shoot the rapids of a changing world but also change modes of transportation midstream. The adolescents' world is changing. While the world around them experiences rapid transition, the adolescent himself or herself is undergoing a metamorphosis. Adolescents enter the adult world in an emerging body of a thirteen-year-old and in seven short years are expected to navigate society as a young adult. No other period of the human developmental cycle is so packed with stressing decisions, alluring temptations, and frightening new responsibilities. The decisions made during adolescence literally affect the remaining decades of one's life, and these decisions must be made at a time when the adolescent is expected to pull back from family and assert his or her independence. While a number of space-age adolescents fail to negotiate the rapids and wind up as statistics in the casualty list of society, more than a few challenge the world around them and come out winners.

Temptations call today's teens like a midway carnival barker. Many "step right up" to "try drugs, sex, and alcohol" and wind up paying for the rest of their lives. Responsibilities for a good education, a good paying job, and the right social skills weigh heavily on some teens who feel "hurried" toward adulthood. Others got pushed into earning money to help support their family, spending time and energy raising younger siblings or caring for their own child. These "children of children" are at great risk in society.

The purpose of this essay is to assist ministers, seminarians, and lay youth leaders to understand the rapidly changing world of the teenage generation and to develop an effective ministry especially to the public-school sector. Public-school adolescents are singled out because they appear at greater risk of being ignored by the religious community.

While adolescents are changing internally their world is shifting around them. Early adolescents (twelve to fourteen years old) undergo major physiological changes which precipitate peer-group realignments, family reactions, and identity concerns. Middle adolescence (ages fifteen, sixteen, and seventeen) seems to be a time of exploration and adventure. This is characterized by testing the limits and capabilities of their new minds and bodies in the context of what they perceive to be outdated rules and guidelines. Middle adolescents who fail to keep their heads above water experience some major crises. Frequently they say, "I didn't expect to get in any real trouble, I just wanted to try it once." Late adolescents (ages eighteen, nineteen, and twenty) begin a period of consolidation and refinement or fail to "shoot the rapids" into young adulthood. They can find their place in society in college, vocational training, a job, or the military service. However, many wander about, lost in the search for identity and security like a ship at sea without flag, rudder, and power. As adolescents change internally their world is changing externally at an ever-increasing speed. Today space-age adolescents seem light years away from adolescents of the 60s and 70s.

The Changing Adolescent Subculture

Those who minister to adolescents are wise to conceptualize the teenage world as a different culture. In approaching adolescents as a separate culture one is more prepared to drop assumptions about youth. Each generation of youth has its own culture. A new youth culture develops in a rapidly changing society like the United States every six to eight years. This new culture has its own language, its own heroes, its own worldview, its own customs, and its own mores.

The first step in effective ministry to those space-age adolescents is to know and understand their particular culture. Ministers who spend only a few hours a week with teenagers in their church are no more aware of the youth culture than a person who blinks frequently can be aware of what it is to be blind. To know the adolescent world one must encounter adolescents "on their turf." Visit adolescents in their homes, invite them into your home, visit their schools for an entire day or longer, attend their recreational events, (such as sports contests, music concerts, and certainly rock concerts), listen to their music, watch their television shows, and eat pizzas at their favorite hangouts. Ride with them as they cruise the streets. Know their world.

If you are to reconceptualize the adolescent world, you should adopt the stance of an anthropologist living in a remote culture. Enter their world as a visitor with awe and respect, as one who learns, not as a rude and ugly tourist ridiculing the natives. Be aware that your presence itself modifies the culture; become as transparent as possible during the learning phase. Only after establishing rapport through knowing the culture can you expect to begin to inform, reform, and transform the youth culture. Like an anthropologist, learn to value the culture and learn from it. Only then can you hope to minister within it. Effective ministry is not to public-school youth as much as it is *with* public-school youth. Until you know them and live with them you cannot minister to them nor organize and equip them to minister to one another.

During the late 1980s I visited five major metropolitan areas and interviewed hundreds of adolescents from various socioeconomic, ethnic, and religious backgrounds. A frequent question that generated rich insights was, "What would you like to say to a group of parents and other adults in order that they might better understand you?" The teenagers spoke freely. While their responses covered a wide range of topics, three or four always seemed to be present. The adolescents would say something like, "Trust that we have a mind of our own and help us to think for ourselves, stop telling us what to do all the time." Another common refrain was, "Listen to us, hear us out, know what we are saying before you respond." A third repeated cry was, "Don't be too quick to judge us. Until you have lived in our world and faced what we face, you don't know how we feel." Another frequent reply was, "Be concerned and care about what happens to us." Adolescents pointed out that the adult generation was polluting their world, using their resources, endangering their future through nuclear irresponsibility and generally not valuing adolescents as persons.

One final word from the adolescent world was a plea for their parents to spend more time with them. These teens did not want their parents to be so busy or isolated or detached through divorce. One girl spoke to this point when she complained, "He divorced my mom, not me." When parents were confronted with the latter response many of them complained that when they tried to spend time with their adolescents that the time was filled with awkward silence or, worse, open rebellion. Perhaps this is because the parents and adolescents live in two different cultures and haven't spent enough time together to communicate effectively and meet needs reciprocally. Rather than avoid such discomfort parents need to reconnect with their youth's world.

Changing Society Influences Adolescents

Social changes of the 70s and 80s impact the adolescents' world dramatically. Today's adolescents live in a world where 60 percent of mothers are employed outside the home, where persons are exploring in space, where someone walking on the moon is ancient history (before their birth), where the average family moves once every three years, where real family life is almost nonexistent, where television introduces them to the adult themes of sex, violence, and greed at a very early age. Because of dual and dueling public and private schools and the mobility of society, adolescent neighborhood peer groups are almost nonexistent in urban areas. Lonely adolescents, who need to belong, are ripe to be exploited by gang leaders, drug kingpins, pimps, or anyone else who makes them feel important.

It appears as if the secularization of the 60s and 70s met with the moral majority backlash of the 80s to produce a polarized society for the last decade of this millennium. The polarization of the 90s confronts the teenage world with diverse options and social choice overload. While a number of contemporary adolescents are responsible, hardworking, intelligent leaders for tomorrow, a major portion of adolescents are in crises.

Exact figure are difficult to come by, but professionals agree that the United States of America now has the highest adolescent pregnancy rate of any Western civilized country, the highest youth alcohol consumption, the highest adolescent suicide rate, the highest participation in drug abuse among youth, and some of the lowest academic scores upon graduation from high school. Today's public school adolescents upon graduation from high school will find a peer culture where approximately one in three use some form of drugs, 50 percent consume alcohol weekly, and from 60-70 percent are sexually active. One secular social researcher has commented that sex for the modern teenager is like a McDonald's hamburger, "easy to find, fast, cheap, and essentially tasteless." With all of the internal and external stress confronting contemporary adolescents, it is no wonder that they are in need of ministry in order to effectively negotiate the rapids in their changing world.

Caring for Adolescents

A few specific adolescent crises will be discussed and general principles for ministering with adolescents suggested. For a detailed discussion of the needs of adolescents see G. Wade Rowatt, *Pastoral Care with Adolescents in Crises* (Westminster Press, 1989) and Richard D. Parsons, *Adolescents in Turmoil—Parents Under Stress* (Paulist Press, 1987). For specific assistance in public-school matters see Helen P. Barnette, *Your Child's Mind: Making the Most of Public Schools* (Westminster Press, 1984).

Personal identity, family tensions, faith queries, substance abuse, sexual matters, school pressures, and depression, and suicide have all been listed by those who minister to youth as major crises faced on a regular basis. In a recent survey by this author of ninety-seven ministers from a variety of denominations across the United States personal identity remains the number-one crisis of adolescents. Contemporary youth not only must find out who they are in a changing body, they must deal with a multitude of social options. The plurality of society brings them into a world of ethnic, racial, and religious diversity so complex that many youth never find an answer to the question "Who Am I?" Before a person can blend with another culture he or she must establish an identity in his or her own culture. Public school students are perhaps faced with this issue more often than their homogeneously grouped private school peers. Certain groups seem to be more at risk. Afro-American males, for example, have few options for defining themselves apart from athletics and music. Those who find a place in the church report a remarkable level of identity stability. Asian-American youth report being so pressured to succeed and get ahead that they are anxious and overstressed. From an early age they receive family pressure to excel academically. Hispanic youth struggle for a sense of empowerment and value in some segments of American society. The thousands of immigrant youth from Third World countries are seeking a place of hope. Surprisingly, many youth of European background record an overwhelming sense of isolation and loneliness because of rapid mobility of society, a lack of trust within communities, and the diversity of schools represented in most churches. Many youth lack a consistent peer group in which to formulate their identity.

Changes in the American family, long overdue in some respects, have meant liberation and personhood for some women and not a few males. Nevertheless, shifting role expectations for males and females have contributed to confusion in dating patterns. Adolescents are still adjusting to these changes of family patterns. It appears that adolescent females fare better than adolescent males, particularly if the boy's father is having difficulty accepting the mother's newfound independence and freedom. Two-career families have less time to support their children in homework. Step-families have fewer resources for working as a blended family and single-parent families are frequently under too much pressure for the parent to be actively involved in the adolescent's education. Adolescents who are wards of the state or live in social institutions frequently have no advocate at all. Ministers can take a stand for adolescents in general but particularly as advocates for those who have no parent to stand by their side.

Alcohol and drug abuse confront adolescents daily. Few if any public high and middle schools are free from alcohol and drug abuse. Many public-school adolescents report daily temptations to use or buy some form of drug or alcohol. Drug- and alcohol-education programs, as well as stepped up enforcement activities, and rehabilitation programs need community support from clergy. Peer pressure remains the number-one factor in teen drug abuse. The church can offer an alternative peer group for community teens. While many clergy are reluctant to get involved in adolescent drug-abuse counseling and rehabilitation, it appears that involvement from caring adults other than one's parents is a significant part of the recovery process.

The sexual revolution is such ancient history that contemporary adolescents are surprised to hear of a world in which four-letter words and sex were not regular menu items on movie screens, in popular magazines, and on television. Adolescents lack adequate sexual information. While they might get some physiological education in the public schools, moral education is still a strong need. I feel that many churches are abdicating their responsibility and refusing to get involved. Not only are traditional problems of pregnancy and sex-abuse important issues, but AIDS has erupted to this generation in mega proportions. See *AIDS in the Church* by Earl Shelp and Ronald Sunderland (Westminster Press, 1987) for additional information.

School problems focus around vocational confusion, lack of adequate study place, habits, and encouragement, but are complicated by the presence of violence in the public schools and the lack of adequate numbers of mentors with whom the adolescent can form a caring alliance. Adolescents need teachers, coaches, Sunday School teachers, ministers, youth ministers, and adult friends who will assist them in monitoring their study habits and encourage them toward excellence.

Adolescents who receive only limited reinforcement frequently fail and become dropouts. Teens need to know that someone cares about their school performance. They desire to be important to someone. The adolescent suicide rate continues to rise. Depression is a major illness among contemporary adolescents. While automobile accidents remain the number-one cause of death among adolescents, suicides are increasing rapidly. Some suicides are related to broken relationships with their parents; however, the primary cause seems to be a lost boyfriend/girlfriend relationship. While ministers know the value of grief counseling during adolescence, most of us miss the opportunity to minister to adolescents during their grief and depression over broken dating relationships. It may seem like puppy-love to us, but it is a life-threatening issue to many adolescents. Getting involved in their lives and assisting them in bonding with family members greatly reduces the changes of suicide.

Concluding Theological Reflections

How does one give youth "a cup of cold water in His name?" Perhaps the most significant ministry one can perform for public school adolescents is to create a "user-friendly" community in which the adolescent can experience support, stability, and energy for the task of "shooting the rapids" into adulthood. While one cannot undergo the transition for an adolescent, a minister can work toward a social environment conducive to and appreciative of adolescents. Ministers can be involved on school boards and as community leaders to see that every adolescent is given the opportunity for an education in the context of a school that cares. Ministers can participate in family-life education programs that strengthen the adolescent's homebase. Furthermore, ministers can stress family values in relationship to other social institutions and can certainly see that our own churches do not inappropriately take people away from their families without thought for the impact on the children and youth in those families.

We can create a business community that is aware of the needs of adolescents—one that seeks on one hand to deal effectively with the need for adolescent jobs and on the other hand does not exploit the adolescent employment market to the point the adolescents cannot be effective students. One study showed that teenagers who work more than fifteen hours per week suffer significant losses in their educational programs. Still many teens need a job with money and respect.

As we create this "user-friendly" community for adolescents we certainly must be involved in building and funding adequate adolescent recreation programs. Adolescents need places to congregate, opportunities to exercise, and programs in which to excel. Adolescents who are actively involved in a recreation league, music program, mission trip, civic service project, or economic venture are more likely to value themselves and less likely to be experimenting their way into a crisis for excitement.

It goes without saying that adolescents need information on such things as sex, drug abuse, and other subjects. Additionally, the legal system needs to be "user friendly" for adolescents, with judges, attorneys, and the police system working to control adolescent experimentation so they will not damage themselves or others and yet encouraging opportunities for adolescents to be rehabilitated rather than started on a life of crime.

How do you share faith with an adolescent? The minister and the community will provide adolescents with a system of faith that has matured beyond a childhood, easy-answers approach. They need a system of hope that does not deny the pain and agony of the world but brings, through faith, opportunities for crises to be transformed into growth. Ministers also bring a message of love grounded in the gospel story. Jesus not only loved the little children of the world but loved and called upon all Christians to love neighbor as self and even enemies.

By permeating the community with a realistic message of faith, hope, and love, ministers provide a foundation and theological framework for adolescents as they encounter enormous change and unavoidable conflict in the passing of time. Ministers who assist adolescents to shoot the rapids effectively must understand the adolescent world, and respond personally, as their shepherd. However, in order to meet the overwhelming needs of the multitudes of adolescents these ministers must become change agents in their community to create an understanding of the adolescent culture and a commitment to provide community resources necessary to meet the basic developmental and crises needs of teenagers.

Forgiveness and reconciliation, two key concepts in any theological system, serve as focal points for a ministry with adolescents and their families. Crises in the early years of life cannot be permitted to relegate an adolescent to years of failure. As we labor to aid adolescents to navigate the troubled waters of their turbulent years, may the image of the father of the prodigal inspire all of us toward forgiveness and reconciliation for those who fail as teens.

||| 12 |||

For the Sake of Love

by J. Alfred Smith, Sr.

Introduction

A paralysis of nostalgia prevents many local churches from reaching their communities with the reconciling action of the gospel of Jesus Christ. Few churches are careful to follow the model of G. Willis Bennett—to examine carefully and skillfully the characteristics and nuances of their communities. Lacking either the sociological tools for evaluating the *"sitz im leben,"* or lacking the passionate magnetism to draw the people in their neighborhoods, these churches brood over how churches used to be filled on Sunday mornings and Sunday evenings. They long for the days when enrollment in Baptist Training Union (Discipleship Training) was nearly as large as in Sunday School.

Plagued with such nostalgia, these churches cannot fully experience the excitement of ministry in these times, pregnant with the reality and challenges of the twenty-first century. They reject the challenges of both present and future days. Such rejection is an easy response to the uneasy feeling of being cut off from the past and is a result of the static security of tradition. This nostalgia manifests not only anxiety of alienation from the past and its now-remembered glories. It also represents a failure to recognize that the world has changed, is changing, and no perfunctory or ritualistic assignment of holy diadems to attitudes and values of the present will arrest the social regression and intense alienation that these churches will experience with their changing communities.

How sad it is that many churches are out of touch with their communities. Preaching a gospel of fantasy and carrying out the rituals from the ecclesiastical archives of the remembered past, these churches justify their lack of rapport with their communities by ascribing to principles of homogeneity among church members. The incarnational reality of God in Christ is thereby rejected. But it should be remembered that it was God in Christ who, for the sake of love, brought redemption, deliverance, wholeness, health, and salvation into a world of cultural and religious pluralism, ethnic diversity, and class stratification. Reaching into any community with the gospel requires an openness that places no absolute value on past methodologies, or methodologies successful in a different setting, or on any universal curriculum provided by the ecclesiastical hierarchy of Christian educators. Instead, for the sake of love, those who make up the memberships of local churches must endeavor to be effective good-news people themselves, before screaming the good news of God's love story to others.

The Absence of Love

Most recently, I was called upon to speak about Dr. Martin Luther King, Jr., at an outstanding California state university. It was an unusually exciting experience. The audience at the university enjoyed a high-school gospel choir and warmly responded to oratorical preaching flights, as I talked about how Jesus Christ was Lord of Dr. King's life of giveness, forgiveness, and nonviolence. Upon leaving the parking lot of the school, I made a wrong turn and ended up in the parking lot of an affluent church nearby. The church was located on prime real estate. It was situated high up in the East Bay hills, overlooking the Oakland-San Francisco Bay. Contrasting this pastoral view was an ugly reality. The church buildings were locked and no car was on the parking lot but mine. From where I sat, the view seemed almost surreal, for, alas, below this pastoral scene was a hungry, homeless, and crime-ridden community at the foot of the hills. At the foot of the hills were people in need and what the church high on the hill was called to give them, all for the sake of love.

In travels across America I have often seen affluent churches that, for the most part, open only on Sunday. In some instances, none of the neighbors attend any of the worship services, nor do they know the names of the pastors or any of the members. These churches, not for the sake of love, but for the sake of their existence as exclusive, ecclesiastical country clubs for their chosen members, are invisible six days a week. These churches are held in comfortable, self-imposed captivity to their in-group prejudices.

Is it too judgmental and harsh for me to castigate and excoriate churches who are introverted in their relationships to their communities? Could I not soften my criticisms by ascribing their behavior to unfortunate theological presupposition? For ideological perceptions and culturally conditioned concepts of biblical interpretation color the theological views that churches hold about doctrine and ministry. Let us examine how theology, when distorted, can innocently motivate churches to relate to their communities with no thought for the sake of love.

Theologies of Distortion

Classical theological viewpoints as taught in seminaries, divinity schools, colleges, and universities are not included in my definition of the theology of distortion. It would be grossly unfair to penalize higher Christian education for the introversion and myopia that define the relationship of many pastors and churches to their communities. To do so would countenance antiintellectualism. I am reminded of the unpleasant antiintellectualism of many clergy and laypersons in their views toward using the insights of theology and the social sciences as an interdisciplinary methodology for properly relating to their community, for the sake of love. What are these facts? The narrow bibliolatry, the antipathy for hermeneutics and exegesis, the fear of truth that sometimes comes from the womb of secularity—such as the diagnostic truths of social sciences, and the fear that seminary education is antithetical to the leadership of the Holy Spirit are all true signs of the virus of antiintellectualism. I label such antiintellectual distortion "folk theology." Any folk theology based on narrow cultural relativism and sectionalized empiricisms lack the objectivity and correction that come from classical, historical, theological traditions. How long will these folk theologians impede the progress of churches who should responsibly relate to their community for the sake of love?

Approximately five schools of thought are very vocal in folk theology. They are:

1. Each local church is a service center or filling station for the clientele designated by denomination, tradition, custom, national or ethnic group.

2. Each local church grows when it is a homogenous unit. Class and cultural conformity are more important for institutional success than color conformity.

3. Each local church is a preaching station where people come to hear the gospel. The people must come to the church (not the church to the people). Outreach programs, ministry to people's needs, and programs to raise the socioeconomic levels are good of themselves, but the priority of each local church is to save lost souls by only preaching the gospel.

4. Each local church is an island of righteousness in a sea of sinful secularity. Pastor Brown must remain silent in the pulpit on community or civic issues of a controversial nature. Pastor Brown will be allowed to support the principalities and powers that control government policy because these principalities and powers, by virtue of their existence, are ordained by God. Power, wealth, and influence in society are rewards of hard work and a deep and abiding loyalty to the Protestant ethic. Sinful secularity is the root cause of poverty and social catastrophe. Hence, each church should maintain the status quo and enjoy the privilege as an island of righteousness in a sea of sinful secularity.

5. Each local church must work not to change the community but to change each individual. The "nonspiritual" problems of those who

live in the sinful body are of no practical concern to the suburbanite. This is not a problem for the suburban church because if the central city pastor would preach a born-again gospel to each individual in the inner-city neighborhood, soon visible changes would take place in the central city. The preacher must not preach against apartheid in South Africa, nor must the membership ask the denominational agencies or their pension boards to divest of their economic holdings in banks that do business in South Africa, because unconscious or conscious economic transactions by church members will have no adverse effect on black South Africans. Each black South African needs most of all the gospel, not justice. You cannot save the community. Just save the individual soul for life after death, and the problems of life after birth should be left to the poor victims to solve, notwithstanding their legacy of powerlessness, poverty, and pitiable plight of education. Yet status-quo churches with a folk theology *can and will* be adversely affected by sociological and economic realities over which they fail to exercise any control or influence.

Sociological and Economic Realities

Aging congregations with declining memberships are usually introverted memberships, struggling either to survive or postpone the day of demise. Such congregations do not have the energy, resources, or personnel necessary to minister to their communities. Some of these churches are transitional churches. If the ethnic composition of the communities change, some of these churches, in an act of desperation for survival, for the first time invite persons of the now-dominant ethnic minority to pastor their churches. Sometimes women ministers are given poor opportunities to be spiritual superpersons for churches not expected to survive. Their charge is resuscitive—to breathe life into churches that are nearly dead. Often, the "solution" for struggling Anglo churches is simply to close their doors or relocate, because the community's ethnic makeup has changed, and any evangelism that ever existed abruptly stops at the color or class line, as a matter of policy and practice. Such action surely is not for the sake of love, but it is for the sake of perverse denominational identity and power. In spite of such sinful, human motivations, God sometimes performs miracles in these situations and resurrects these churches. They are resurrected as they transform their communities with the message and mission of the Christian gospel.

Congregations should not be so fearful that they allow rapid social changes to result in the debilitating, if not crippling, illness of nostalgia. Times that were are often not better than times that are. New challenges in this day provide new opportunities for ministry. Rather than romanticizing the past as a golden age, the past should be seen as the Eden for which it is, to which there is no return. Whether we accept it or not, we are here in *these* days and the responsibility for handling these days lies with us. The stewards of days past had to deal with the difficult of their times, just as we have to deal with ours today. (There is some irony in our yearning for "the good old days," because the contemporaries of the good old days yearned for them, too. The late great comedienne Jackie "Moms" Mabley put it best when she used to say, "Everybody's always talkin' about the good old days. I was there; where were they?")

Today's challenges and what we do with them for the future should be exciting. We should be excited about hearing the voice of the high calling of God in Christ for churches to come boldly into the twenty-first century with the faithfulness of Abraham. With this faith, we are to pioneer a path and a place for coming generations. We must pass on to the coming generation the sum and substance of our faith to enable them to keep God's new covenant as they wait for a city whose builder and maker is God. The love of God for us does not call for less.

For Love's Sake

The Reverend Larry Rose and Dr. G. Willis Bennett challenged the Allen Temple Baptist Church of Oakland, California, and its pastors to study our community and search for ways to improve our structure and style in order to better serve our community. They worked carefully and critically with us. They challenged us to study ourselves as a church as well as our community, city, and the East Bay megapolis. Rose and Bennett advised us of our need for more professionally trained people on the pastoral staff to assist me in my work. They encouraged us to continue utilizing over 200 laypersons and conducting over forty programs of community ministry. They led us in the process of establishing short-range and long-range goals. They helped us to provide an accountability system of continuing evaluation. They challenged us to be open to new challenges and to employ new methods for meeting them. They enabled us to redefine community so that lay volunteers are active and aggressive in overseas mission work as volunteers in Third World countries.

As a result of the classic textbook written by G. Willis Bennett, *Effective Urban Church Ministry: A Case Study of the Allen Temple Baptist Church*, I am often invited to lecture at conferences, colleges, universities, seminaries, and churches. I can expect one peculiar request during every question-and-answer session. This request always misses the basis for effective church ministry, because every group seems to want a ready-made program, instant formula, or package of ideas on how to serve *their* community. They say, "Tell us what to do." In response, I always ask the same questions: Do you love the people in your community? Do you sit with them? Do you rejoice with them? Do you listen to them? Do they tell you what their needs are? Were you there when one of their young died of a drug overdose? Were you present when a son or daughter graduated from school with honors? Were you responsive when the social worker needed help in understanding the Asian or Hispanic culture? Did you participate with other pastors from other churches in an ecumenical project to help AIDS victims, or did your denominational piety and your unconscious theological arrogance isolate you from the community and persons who are to the left of you, right of you, or "below" you? (Did not Jesus die between two thieves?) Are denominational politics more important than your standing at a modern Calvary with a nonbeliever either at your ideological right or left? If you are not prepared for risk, then the community will know that you serve not for the sake of love.

Conclusion

You and I should say with the late Sister Fanny Lou Hamer, "We are sick and tired of being sick and tired." We are sick and tired of playing church and of talking about the gospel as if our lectures, conferences, books, research, and writings are the deed. Love says: Be good-news people, do good news, tell good news. The first step of being is ontological. The second step of doing is existential. The third step of telling good news is proclamational. Love is not working until these three dimensions are harmonized, concretized, and actualized.

Love calls us to a modern Calvary in our communities. Calvary is not what we verbalize, romanticize, or theologize, but what we actualize. Some of us in central cities have been physically brutalized as we stood up against drug pushers. Some of us, in the words of the old Negro spiritual, have been " 'buked, we have been scorned, we have been lied on, we have been called everything but a child of God." We have been criticized not only by sinners outside the membership of the local churches, but we have also been criticized and castigated by self-righteous church members who forget that they are just sinners saved by grace. We became good news, did good-news work, and preached the good news of God's grace to persons with AIDS and to others outside of the camp of conformity, acceptability, and respectability. But this we must do. Yes, we must do this for the sake of love.

As Old Testament scholar Abraham Heschel once said, love invites us:

> [T]o be in travail with God's dreams and designs, God's dreams of a world redeemed, of reconciliation of heaven and earth, of a [humankind] which is truly His image, reflecting His wisdom, justice and compassion.[1]

Love invites us, as Otis Moss, has written:

> [T]o convert oppression into poetry, exploitation into creative force, humiliation into hunger for justice, haunting fears into hymns of faith.[2]

These words of Otis Moss describe the historical past and present of

African-American Baptist churches. Whereas Anglo Southern Baptist churches may not readily identify with the poetic imagery of the lyrical theology of African-American cultural heritage, those who represent power, privilege, and the cream of aristocratic theological refinement, are challenged to hear theologian A. Durwood Foster remind Christocentric thinkers that:

> The vision of the supremacy of Christ-like love is still pregnant with creative implications for Western [people] as well as for the future of the whole world.[3]

Sake is but another word for purpose. *Love* is but another word for Christ. Those purposed in Christ must *effectively* carry out His agenda, for the sake of love.

Notes

1. Abraham J. Heschel, *Who Is Man?* (Stanford, Ca.: Stanford University Press, 1965), 119.
2. Otis Moss, "Black Church Distinctives," in Emanuel McCall, *The Black Christian Experience* (Nashville, Tn.: Broadman Press, 1972), 15.
3. A. Durwood Foster, *The God Who Loves* (New York: Collier-McMillan Limited, 1971), 5.